GLASS HALF-FULL

Lucy Rocca

In at the Deep End – August 1st 2012

Here's where I'm at: sixteen months ago I had my last drink. I didn't particularly want to stop drinking but rather felt that if I didn't, I might die. You see, for me, alcohol has never been a substance that I could consume in moderation, and on most occasions when I made the unwise decision to crack open a bottle of pinot grigio (or chablis if I was feeling posh) I proceeded to get horribly drunk.

Drinking has landed me in no end of trouble over the course of the last two decades, from initiating belligerent arguments to making unwise choices in boyfriends to engaging in regrettable episodes of public dancing and wild, unfettered flirting with people I most definitely should not have flirted with.

These are just some of the reasons behind my decision to end my relationship with booze back in April last year. It hasn't been all bad, this sober living business, but I have to admit there has been many a moment when I would have killed for a cold glass of white wine, or willingly run naked through a busy city centre for the chance of a secret rendezvous with a bottle of red – but I haven't. Something inside stopped me: fear maybe, or perhaps merely a will to change that has overwhelmed my long-standing desire to self-destruct.

I know I'm not alone in this, my internal battle against the cravings and lusting after that old favourite, the self-medicating liquid that promises so much and dangles glamour and relaxation before our very eyes, only to veer off wildly to a place far more sinister once a few glasses have slipped down. It can't just be me, who never knows when she has had enough and should call it a night, brush her teeth, and sensibly imbibe sufficient water to ward off the evils of the hangover the next day, can it?

I desperately want to understand myself and undergo a mental shift which will see me transported from where I'm at now (grudgingly accepting the fact that I am, all of a sudden, a boring non-drinker who fears the word 'fun' is no longer a part of her vernacular) to someone who is happy and confident and devoid of the urge to drink away her emotions at the drop of a hat.

There are numerous elements of alcohol-free life that I love; the hangover-free mornings, the level mood, the brighter eyes, the lack of car-crash situations that spin out of control and impact on so much, and so many, around me. But in the background there is always the niggling worry that I'll never be able to let my hair down again and that, somehow, this pace of life just isn't *me*. If only I could learn to drink 'responsibly', to moderate, to sprout that elusive off-switch. However, experience, unfortunately, has taught me this will never happen.

I'm thirty-six years old, engaged to Sean, and mother to two lovely girls. I don't know if I am an alcoholic or not – I'm not sure I even know what an alcoholic is. I don't know if I will ever be happy to be a non-drinker, and I have no idea of how I will turn out without my beloved crutch of wine. What I do know is that there has to be a better way than spending the remainder of my days gritting my teeth and obstinately rebuffing alcohol while inside I'm desperately craving a drink. In writing this blog, I want to work through my feelings and help myself find where I want to be – who knows, it may just help others too.

This, then, is my journey.

Biscuits v Pinot Grigio – August 2nd 2012

About twelve months ago I became pregnant, and from the moment that I peed on a stick and witnessed the blue cross appear in the window I began to eat and eat like there was no tomorrow. Happily morning sickness wiped out the cravings for booze. However, in their place came the most impossible-to-ignore desire for pizza, bread, cheese and pickle, lard (not really, but my hips and arse wouldn't have known that for their dramatic increase in girth), ice cream and BISCUITS. Lots of biscuits. Faster than you could say 'bun in the oven' I had clapped on about a stone and a half, and it only got worse from there.

Before I became pregnant and sober, I hardly touched sugary food, choosing instead to consume the bulk of my weekly calorie intake in alcohol. Somehow I managed to maintain a reasonable weight of nine and a half stone (I attempted to counteract the booze problem with a bit of running, fooling myself into believing that it would negate my being an ardent boozer), but then again I picked at food like an old woman and had an unnatural ability to control my cravings for fatty and sweet foods. Alas, now that the booze has been eliminated and the bun has been cooked and served fresh from the oven, the sweet cravings have not subsided one jot.

I was led to believe that one of the more pleasing side effects of saying sayonara to booze was that the pounds would drop off rapidly, leaving a newly sober person to reap the rewards of her impressive rejection of alcohol by way of a svelte, fat-free figure. I have to be honest – this has not been the case. Yes, I did have a baby a few weeks ago, and yes I stuffed my face like a fat-camp escapee at a pie-eating contest for nine months, but still … I had kinda hoped that a satisfying amount of post-pregnancy weight loss could be achieved with minimum effort in the gym and by refusing that second packet of chocolate digestives, simply because I was no longer getting sozzled several nights a week. Not so.

It would unfortunately appear that biscuits and chocolate have replaced my addiction to alcohol. Definitely not as damaging to myself, my liver, family, and society at large, but if I want to shed this last stone and a half before our family holiday to Mallorca in four weeks' time then I have to get my biccie-munching under control. Pathetic as it sounds, those sweet treats have become one of the few remaining vices in my life (actually, my only vice). Would it be possible to live happily with no vices at all? Now there's a thought …

Relight My Fire (starter) – August 5th 2012

Since Lily, my youngest, was born, I became (all at the same time) babysitter, washerwoman, cleaner, and general dogsbody, while getting paid virtually nothing (Statutory Maternity Pay is pretty shoddy). Simultaneously, I have been attempting to tone up my sadly neglected body and maintain my relationship with baby's father, which has most definitely been put on the backburner since her arrival. And I'm not just referring to sex – we have barely spoken in weeks. This has not been through want of trying, or because we hate each other, but because any exchanges that have occurred between us have generally taken place as we run between rooms clutching dirty nappies/armfuls of laundry/a baby/our dinner, or as we lie comatose in bed, relishing the silence and the lack of demands that are being placed upon us. Neither scenario is supportive of a healthy, vigorous sex life.

In order to combat this situation, it struck me that what might have been nice (in another life) would be to get the baby in bed, crack open a bottle of merlot, and snuggle up on the settee to watch a DVD. This is not an option, due to one shared bottle of merlot inevitably leading to another one, maybe two, followed by a quick scouring of the kitchen cupboards to seek out any remnants of old liqueurs and spirits that might be lurking, left over from parties or from the occasional foray into a Nigella or Jamie book. After necking all available booze on the premises, the CD collection would get a good thrashing, I would dance raver-circa-1990 style around the living room before crashing out on the settee about 3 a.m. and waking up with the most horrific hangover, only to find myself back in the real world of babysitter/washerwoman/etc. (please refer to the above paragraph).

My other half goes out once a week, and imbibes a bit of alcohol. I don't grumble about this but I do insist that he sleeps in the spare room on his return, due to excess beer-drinking causing him to snore like a sleeping troll. But we do not drink together, and I miss it. When the daily grind and stresses come to a close early in the evening, it cannot be denied that one of life's pleasures is the sharing of a quality bottle of wine with one's loved one, often leading to one of life's other pleasures: the sharing of each other's bodies in the sack. Somehow, a pot of tea and several McVitie's Boasters don't have quite the same effect.

Drinking alcohol is a fast-track way to relaxation, and when time is at a premium, fast-track is what is called for. I also used to drink (too much) because booze has a wonderful way of instantly making me feel more sexy, interesting, and fun. And, let's face it, when you're slobbing in front of the TV in your trackies, biscuit in hand and crumbs down your top, you need all the help you can get in that department. And so it has dawned on me that whereas, for some people, alcohol provides an easy route to relaxation, I need to draw on other methods.

Maybe some sexy underwear, a massage, and an early night together would do the trick. One thing I do know, there is nothing sexy about a thirty-something mother-of-two dancing on the coffee table to 'Firestarter' before throwing up on the carpet. Yes, that once was me …

Social Sloth – August 6th 2012

I have no social life. This is in part due to the fact that I had a baby three months ago and for the weeks that I spent heavily pregnant (and the size of a large building) I had absolutely no inclination to leave the house, other than to walk the dog in a half-arsed attempt to work off a few biscuit calories. So I sort of got accustomed to being a homebody, and really rather preferred being slumped in front of *Grand Designs* to lumbering around some bar in a badly fitting maternity frock, drinking mineral water and being stared out sympathetically by the other clientele. ("Oh, poor thing, isn't she huge! She must be ready to pop any minute now …").

The weight is still something of an issue (a stone left to lose) but not so bad that I feel like a freak show whenever I'm out in public. The issue is that I have no idea how to have fun in a social situation when I'm sober, and rather than try to learn, I'm finding it easier to hide in the living room with Kevin McCloud.

I stopped drinking sixteen months ago, and in that time I have been out socially on two occasions. Yes, two. And I've noticed that of late I have become a bit of a misery guts when it comes to other people enjoying themselves, especially when they do so under the influence of booze. For instance, last night I was woken up at 2 a.m. by a bunch of girls falling out of a taxi outside our house. They then proceeded to dissect the night's events for the next half an hour in voices like foghorns directly beneath our window. I lay in bed listening to them and wishing I could lay my hands on a handful of rotten tomatoes to chuck out of the Velux.

I walk past signs advertising alcohol outside bars – 'Why

not stop and enjoy a refreshing cocktail?' – and I feel my eyes narrow in disdain, my lips pursing together as I go all Presbyterian on the world. I glare when somebody smokes within a hundred metres of me, expressing my disapproval loudly just like my mum used to do when she was trying to put me off cigarettes when I was younger.

And it is pretty hypocritical, all of this disgust I feel towards people who smoke and drink and socialise. Up until sixteen months ago, I could be found sitting outside my local in all weathers (heated and covered outdoor stable yard, great for chain-smoking in tandem with necking vast quantities of booze!) several nights a week, or bar-hopping between cool establishments filled with glamorous people, sipping champagne cocktails and feeling oh-so-sophisticated (until I fell over on the way out, stumbling in my efforts to stand up again in my stupidly high stilettos).

So why do I feel as though all of this is out of my reach, now that I no longer befriend Mr Pinot Grigio? After much soul-searching, I have come to the conclusion that the reasons are as follows:

a) I don't know who I am. In certain social situations (i.e. evening, where everyone else is drinking alcohol, and in public places) I just don't know how to act without the prop of wine. It's easy to pull on a veneer when you drink – the personality just falls into place as the cold, crisp liquid runs down your throat, warming your insides and reaching the part of you that can't come to the surface when sober. Brimming with confidence, witty, knowledgeable – at least to begin with anyway; as the night wears on a different face would appear – heavy eyelids, blanked out expression, fixed smile – my mind would shut down as I drift into my own little blanketed world of security, a place where nobody else ever came with me. But sober, I am a completely different kettle of fish. A bit shy, not very confident. Sometimes I can't get my words out and I stutter a little, especially in front of people who I don't know or who make me feel nervous. I don't feel worthy, I don't feel interesting. I have nothing to say.

b) I feel unattractive and plain when I am not drinking. Even before the first sip of wine had its effect on my brain, I would begin to feel a frisson of excitement and sexiness just at the thought of what lay ahead. And when I had the glass in hand, everything came together, I felt complete. In my hand I clutched magic, something which turned me from a plain Jane into the most fabulous woman in any room. Without it I'm just, well, the same as everyone else.

c) I hate watching other people drink. Hate it, with a passion.

d) Conversations are hard work for me when sober – I have to try a lot harder and often I get easily bored. Alcohol must have smoothed over an awful lot of boorish behaviour, and I thought everyone I spoke to was wildly interesting. In the cold reality of sobriety, this is, sadly, not so.

These are some of the reasons why a night out no longer appeals. Oh yes, and I'm breastfeeding, which gives me the perfect excuse to keep up-to-date with *Grand Designs* for a few more weeks yet. Come the autumn, however, I will have to think of a new one – or learn how to enjoy socialising when sober ...

Robert the Geranium Plant – August 9th 2012

I am not a scientist by any stretch of the imagination. At the tender age of fourteen, I was told by my physics teacher that I would never get anywhere in life because I didn't know how a radiator worked. And that Robert, a geranium plant which sat on the classroom windowsill, had more brain cells than me. Incidentally, I believe the theories of a man who names his geranium plant Robert deserve no credence, but hey, I digress. I do, however, have a theory regarding the way that alcohol prevents people from reaching emotional maturity, should they do as I did and consume vast amounts of the stuff from mid-teens onwards.

I have grown up more in the last sixteen months since becoming teetotal than I did in all the years prior to that turning point. When I cast an eye back to my booze-obsessed self, I see someone who prioritised alcohol above everything else, including, I am ashamed to say, my elder daughter, and whose main aim, in absolutely every endeavour I engaged in, was to get pissed. Sister's wedding; get hammered. Friend's 40th birthday party; get wasted. New Year's Eve party with the kids; get the little ones in bed ASAP and then hit the wine, big time. All that drinking left me with very little time to grow as a person, and now that I've been sober for a year and a half I'm all too aware of the fact that I didn't mature emotionally until very recently.

Since giving up alcohol, I think more about how others feel. I consider how my actions will affect them, and then I adjust my behaviour accordingly in order to make their lives better. Now I realise that this sounds like pretty fundamental stuff, but my emotional development froze somewhere around the arsey, self-obsessed fifteen-year-old girl stage, when my only concerns in life were which boy I fancied/ fancied me, Morrissey, smoking, and getting pissed at the weekend when my mum and dad thought I was at the cinema. From that point onwards, I placed drinking ahead of everything and everyone. I never dealt with heartache or regret as I chose instead to smother it with the analgesic quality of booze. I never really experienced true happiness because I was always pie-eyed whenever I was (supposedly) having a good time, and I never knew what a nice feeling could be achieved through truly loving others and committing a selfless act because you place someone else's happiness above your own.

Not only was I emotionally unavailable to everyone in my life, I was a grumpy bugger too. Being hungover most days and surviving on poor quality sleep, together with having chronically low self-esteem as a result of all the awful, stupid things I used to do when I was drunk, meant that I snapped at the most innocent of comments and was generally not very nice to be around.

I wish I could turn the clock back to have been a better mum to my elder daughter during her younger years, but all I can do now is plough my efforts into being the best I can for her and her new little sister, now and in the future. It's so much nicer going to bed at night when you are proud of what you have achieved that day, instead of beating yourself up because of the never-ending shit that you inflict on the people who love you. My physics teacher was wrong for saying that I would never get anywhere in life; I just took a while getting there.

Out of My Tree – August 10th 2012

A few weekends ago, we (me and my family) wandered down to the local park which was playing host to a folk festival as part of the wider 'Tramlines' event, a free musical extravaganza in Sheffield, where I live. I was aware of a calmness that I definitely did not possess when I drank, and I began to consider what has changed that makes me quite a different person altogether in the way that I approach life.

In the drinking days I remember there being a knot of fear in my stomach in the run-up to going out socially, an adrenaline-fuelled rush of anxiety brought on by the excitement of not knowing how the night/day would pan out. It was reckless, like standing on a precipice, on the verge of jumping into blackness, unaware of what lay in the void before me. There I would be, watching *Neighbours* and eating my dinner, perfectly in control of my mind and my actions but all the while having the knowledge that in a few hours I would be out of it, impulsive, a different person engaging in situations that I couldn't possibly imagine in my sober mind.

And walking down to the park a few Sundays ago, that familiar route walked every day with my partner, my daughters, and my dog, along the well-worn cobbled paths that I have manoeuvred the pram over so often, I became conscious of the fact that there was no precipice waiting for me. There lay the difference – I knew how the afternoon would go, roughly. The knot of fear had dissipated along with the bottles of wine; without alcohol in the equation, the recklessness doesn't exist.

Compare and contrast:

In summer 2004, I went to the Red Hot Chili Peppers gig

in Hyde Park with my then boyfriend. The gates opened mid-afternoon and following visits to a number of pubs *en route* to the park we eventually arrived, me somewhat the worse for wear. Following an opening act by the late James Brown, during which we continued to drink pint after pint of lager in the hot June sun, the Chilis finally came on. As they appeared on the distant stage I hoisted myself onto my boyfriend's shoulders and proceeded to dance, as only girls at festivals dance, arms flailing in the air, beer in one hand and cigarette in the other. After a few seconds of this, I lurched forward and fell to the hard, stony ground, my face meeting the floor with a resounding smack.

Embarrassed, I stumbled to my feet and attempted to dance, ignoring the concerned voices around me which eventually subsided as it became apparent that I was not about to acknowledge what had just happened, despite the blood that was dripping down the side of my face. Around this stage in the afternoon my memory fades completely (I think this is rather due to the fact that I had drunk God knows how much lager, rather than any indication of concussion, but who knows?) All I do remember is that I had an argument with my boyfriend and wandered off to find other people with whom to continue my one-woman wrecking ball mission.

Hours later, I awoke sitting under a tree in the dark night air on a small hill somewhere in Hyde Park. In front of me were three or four policemen, together with a crowd of people who had gathered around to see what was going down with this strange, drunken woman who was lying semi-comatose beneath an old oak tree. After shaking free of the police and (I have no idea how I achieved this) convincing them that I was fine, I miraculously spotted my boyfriend amongst the throngs of people leaving the gig and wandered towards him, feeling in my pockets as I did so and discovering that I had lost both my mobile phone and purse. Needless to say, the experience drove a stake in to the heart of that relationship and two months later we split up for good. He now lives in Australia.

The alternative scenario plays out by way of a much more pleasing afternoon. The sun was out, it had stopped raining for the first time in weeks, and the baby slept in her pram. We meandered between stalls and folk bands and singers, drank a couple of coffees in the warm, July air, listened to music, and chatted about nothing much. Afterwards I remembered everything. My bloke didn't run off to Australia. My baby wasn't traumatised by having a drunken lush for a mother.

OK, so this version lacks a little of the drama; the police didn't materialise, blood didn't flow. But given the choice, I am happy to live with a little less drama.

Can I Borrow Your Old Smiths T-Shirt Please? – August 12th 2012

Today I broke my own rule and weighed myself five days ahead of my planned weigh-in day. I am one pound less than I was yesterday when I also broke my once-a-week-weigh-in rule, stepping on the scales six days too soon. Before I got pregnant a year ago, I was 134 pounds; currently I am 148 pounds, so a stone to lose. To add insult to injury, I tried on my bikinis last night in order to ascertain whether new ones should be bought prior to our holiday to Mallorca in two and a half weeks' time. Yes, the answer is yes, they most definitely should.

This morning, as I dressed in the only pair of trousers I own that fit comfortably (elasticated waist, stretch denim fabric that squeezes the flesh a little, magically giving the appearance of slimmer legs) and a baggy top that doesn't cling to the spare tyre around my middle, my beautiful and slim thirteen-year-old daughter wafted into the bedroom and asked, 'Mum, can I have that Smiths T-shirt that you never wear any more please?' Of course she could have it – no point clinging on to something that would barely conceal even one of my enormous, breastfeeding boobs.

She takes it, returning presently wearing the T-shirt and looking stylish and young in it. I focus my mind on planning a low-fat day; bananas, yoghurt, no bread, skip the lattes and cakes.

I last wore that T-shirt in April last year, when I was newly sober. I hadn't been out of the house for weeks, consumed as I was by shame and self-hatred owing to the fact that on a particular night in April I drank so much wine I collapsed on the pavement outside my house and was taken to hospital by a passing acquaintance. That night, as they say, was my rock bottom.

A few weeks later my boyfriend put on a Smiths night at his local pub and I felt as though I should show my face by way of support. I had a fringe cut in to my hair in an effort to alter myself, and I wore the Smiths T-shirt. It was tight even then and I felt conspicuous, regretful of my new haircut as I walked into the pub, about to meet many of his friends for the first time. I was the only non-drinker in the room and clutched my mineral water, terrified and uncertain of how I should behave now that I no longer poured wine down my neck.

As the night wore on, drunken behaviour came to the fore. I retreated into the dark corners of the room, hoping nobody would speak to me and wishing time would hurry along. When things wound to a close I raced to the car and drove us home, replacing that T-shirt with pyjamas the instant I reached the sanctuary of our bedroom.

Not long after that night I got pregnant, and so for the last twelve months I have had the perfect excuse for being on the wagon. However, in a few weeks I will no longer be breastfeeding my baby. I will shrink a little in the breast department, the weight will continue to fall off, and I will be back to where I was last April; sober, simply because I have chosen to be that way rather than by nature dictating my lifestyle.

Will I be that person again, the one in the corner wearing the slightly too-tight Smiths T-shirt and hoping against hope that nobody talks to her, that no one asks her why she isn't having a proper drink? I like to think not – that a year's passing has equipped me with a few good reasons as to why I now choose to live life without alcohol propping me up, why my focus has necessarily shifted from a selfish pursuit of getting wasted to the happiness and wellbeing of my family and friends and myself.

In late spring last year, I was emerging from two decades of hiding behind a large glass of white wine and attempting to relocate a personality that wasn't moulded by alcohol. Now, in August 2012, I am a mother for the second time, I am enjoying being alive, I have (almost) eradicated the shame that lingered after years of self-abuse. Today I feel like a proper human being, and it's great.

The Rise of the Soberista – August 13th 2012

After reading an article today, 'The Rise of the Teetotal Generation,'[1] I was reminded once again of why being teetotal is not, and should not be, something to be slightly embarrassed about. Despite being utterly committed to life as a Soberista, I still find myself tongue-tied in social situations whenever anyone I don't know very well asks me what I want to drink, and I know that I am soon to be faced with a barrage of questions about why I don't want something alcoholic.

"Oh, are you driving?"

---

[1] *The Independent Online*, 6th July 2011.

"No."

"Well, why don't you want a drink then?"

"Err, I just don't. I've got a lot on tomorrow."

"Well, just have one then. Come on – what will it be; G & T, a white wine?"

"No really. I don't want a drink because the last time I had a drink I ended up collapsing on the pavement, being taken to hospital, and waking up at 3 a.m. with absolutely no knowledge of what had happened to me, only that I was covered in vomit and that I must never touch alcohol again. So, thanks for the offer, but I'll just have a water."

That's what I want, but find myself unable, to say. However, when I read about the likes of Daniel Radcliffe being on the wagon (see *The Independent* article referenced above), or meet someone who admits to having a drink problem and who has subsequently given it up, the last thing I think is that they are in some way at fault, that they have been weak or have failed at life. Conversely, I regard such people as being brave for fighting a battle that I consider to be one of the hardest there is – to fight against yourself is truly an uphill struggle that never really ends. People who have fought an addiction are, in my mind, heroes.

And yet when it comes to me being honest and giving someone a simple explanation as to why I don't drink alcohol, I have faltered every time.

The first time I was asked why I wasn't drinking was at a party. A rugby-playing, beer-swilling bloke cornered me and wouldn't leave the issue alone (clearly, my mineral water offended his rugby-coloured view of the world), resulting in me being a bit stroppy with him. It wasn't a satisfactory response, and it left me wondering how I should answer the next time such a situation occurred.

Well, the same situation did not occur for a while after that – about ten months actually, as being pregnant gives you a pretty *bona fide* excuse for knocking booze on the head. As I am breastfeeding, I had expected to be able to avoid this dreaded question for a further few months after giving birth, although I have found that generally it is considered acceptable to have a few drinks while nursing (probably not while nursing, as in not holding the baby to breast with one hand and clutching a pint of Stella in the other, but during the nursing period. Most women I have spoken to about this admit to having the odd glass of wine).

And so, there it was again, the big issue, just six weeks after Lily was born. I met a fellow new mother for coffee and she asked me, pointedly, "Have you had a glass of wine yet? Are you drinking while breastfeeding?" Now, this woman is a colleague, so the answer that I had semi-rehearsed in my head after Rugby Boy had questioned my beverage choice was not so appropriate; "No, I don't drink because I am an alcoholic who has decided to live without alcohol ruining my life. I used to drink and whenever I had one it would lead to ten, or however many it took until I passed out. I was ruining my daughter's and my lives and I came to the conclusion that you only live once and I wasn't going to stuff up my life (and my daughter's) by getting shit-faced every night." Because you just can't be that honest with someone you work with.

Or can you? I'm sure that Daniel Radcliffe and his honest confessions about having an alcohol dependency have not gone unnoticed by all the film producers out there. Would they not hire him because of his drinking history next time he springs to their minds as being perfect for a particular role? Of course not, but then again, your choice of actor would be drastically reduced if you discriminated against all those with addictions, past or present. Is it different in the real world? Am I unusual for admiring people who have fought an addiction?

I have come to the conclusion that in social situations I will give an honest answer if questioned about why I don't drink (maybe not completely honest, I'll leave out the bit about waking up in a hospital bed covered in puke) but I will explain that I could not stop drinking once I started and that I had a problem with it. I will say that my life is better without alcohol, for me and for those around me, and that I am far happier without it.

I think that if anyone feels uncomfortable with that as a response, then he or she is probably not a person with whom I would get along anyway.

Wonderful World (but not for Our Neighbours) – August 15th 2012

Last weekend, I experienced two events which confirmed I am definitely beating my booze problem. After feeding the baby, I left her in bed with her dad (he was delighted to be woken at 6.30 a.m. by his Lycra-clad missus) and departed with the dog for a run in the park. Although I am no longer considered to be postpartum by the medical profession (apparently six to eight weeks is when you have to ditch that excuse), it is still necessary in my opinion not to rush things on the exercise front. Thus my route is approximately two miles long and, for the most part, flat as a pancake.

The sun was shining and all was well with the world as I ran alongside a large duck pond, the dog unusually well behaved at my side. My gaze fell on the heron which is often seen stalking the shallows of the ponds in my local park, his beady eyes scanning the water for fish. I felt a surge of happiness for, well, being alive, I guess. Not a soul was in sight other than me, the dog, the heron, and a few ducks quacking in the shady far reaches of the water. Oh, and Craig, the homeless man who has been residing in the park for about ten years and who, last week in the pouring rain, wolf-whistled me. As I ran past him slumbering in his sleeping bag and clutching an oversized bottle of strong cider, I must confess that (despite the alcohol-addled mind of the whistler) I was pretty chuffed to receive this approval so soon after giving birth.

And so there I was, stopping just short of singing a quick rendition of Louis Armstrong's 'What a Wonderful World' as I jogged on through the sunshine, and it occurred to me that I would never have felt such happiness if I was still pouring the wine down my neck each night. An alternative universe would have found me lying in bed groaning quietly at the size of my headache, with a sandpaper tongue and skin like a desiccated lizard. Score one point to me, nil points to the sauce.

Eighteen hours later and I was sharply awoken by the sound of thundering footsteps coming through the wall which divides our bedroom and that of our argument-prone neighbours. There followed the most horrendous, violent exchange, the majority of which came from the very drunken mouth of the male. For the next two hours we lay quietly in bed as the row escalated to include death threats and a number of ambiguous thumping sounds. This couple have two children whom I pictured cowering in their beds with pillows clamped over their heads, desperately attempting to drown out the sound of their parents hating each other.

People argue for many reasons, but a sure-fire way to boost an argument from a minor disagreement to an out-of-control orgy of violence is to add alcohol into the equation. The level of destruction that our neighbours subject themselves and those around them to as a result of drinking too much is unimaginable. When I drank regularly, I found myself involved on numerous occasions in arguments, some violent, all of them loud and utterly unnecessary.

Booze made me pig-headed, narcissistic and angry – a terrible combination. Without alcohol in my life I very rarely have disagreements, and when I do I am (usually) in control of my anger. Listening to our neighbours wage war on each other and causing untold harm to their children served to remind me once again why I am better sober. Much better. Score two points to me, nil points to the sauce.

Marmite and *Top Gear* – August 16th 2012

It has occurred to me on more than one occasion that there are things in this life that I don't like very much (including certain people), and that now I am living my life without the prop of alcohol it's not so easy to let that fact slip by unnoticed. People aside, the things I'm not so keen on include (off the top of my head) Marmite, busy shopping centres, the rain, being cold, *Top Gear*, soap operas, gristly sausages. That list was exactly the same when I drank alcohol as it is today, now that I am sober.

The people who I don't like are a completely different matter.

On a night out a couple of years ago, I spent the early part of the evening sitting outside a rather nice Italian bar situated on a leafy Sheffield road with my lovely sister. As the wine flowed, we sparked up a conversation with two women sitting nearby who had overheard our conversation about my law degree (I was, at that time, studying at university) and who were both solicitors. They too were throwing back the white wine.

There was nothing outwardly wrong with this scenario – it was sociable, convivial and friendly. But if one had peeled back the layer of drunkenness it would have become apparent that both these women were complete arseholes, and, if it weren't for the fact that I was half-cut I wouldn't have wanted to spend one minute of my life with either of them. Nevertheless, my sister and I spent much of the next couple of hours listening to their boorish, self-congratulatory ranting with fixed smiles on our faces, laughing in all the right places.

Here's the thing: without alcohol, a) I would never have got talking to them in the first place, and b) if I'd had the misfortune of getting suckered into their worlds, I would have extricated myself pretty sharpish and relocated to a place far, far away. With the booze in my system, however, I didn't just tolerate them, I actually liked them. I liked the fact that they had struck up a conversation with us (wow, successful, glamorous people who really liked me!!), I liked the association that I had with them, that just by sharing their company and being a part of their worlds (obviously so much better than mine) I improved my status by shifting up a notch on the social scale.

I also approved of the fact that here were two professional women who had no issue with downing a few bottles of wine between them of an evening – now if they drank in such a way, did that let me off the hook? Did it mean that we were all alcoholics, or none of us? We proceeded to stick with them for the next couple of hours, them droning on about their glittering legal careers, my sister and I not getting much of a word in edgeways and drinking even more pinot in order to numb our senses further to mask the agonising boredom of the situation.

On countless occasions I have found myself drinking copious amounts to 'deal with' unsatisfactory social situations – unsatisfactory because I really didn't like the people who I was socialising with. For years I counted people as friends who, really, if I'm honest, were complete morons.

Sober, it doesn't take long at all to work out who we

like and want to spend time with, and who we have nothing in common with, is dull, or who is simply a bit of a tosser. Since giving up drinking, I tend to socialise more during the daytime – meeting friends for a coffee, going to town together, taking the kids to a park – and there are absolutely no walls to hide behind. There are no false pretences, no alternative realities being lived out. I meet people whose company I enjoy and everybody is his or her true self without the veneer of alcohol sugar-coating their personalities.

As I've said, when I drank, the purpose behind whatever social event I was attending was not to spend time with friends or family, or to network, or to celebrate someone's wedding or birthday or promotion. It was to get pissed. It was immaterial who was in attendance, because I was there to slip further inside myself, to sink enough booze to break through my outer layers and relax into the inner part of me that remained locked away when I was sober.

Sober, the purpose of social occasions has been brought back to the fore – if it's someone's birthday, then I am there because I like the person and I want to share in celebrating the birthday. If it's a wedding, then I am there because I want to share in the joy of a couple marrying, not so that I can neck all the free champagne that is being handed out, cop-off with some desperate bloke who is not terribly discerning and doesn't mind that his new love interest is puking over the side of the bed, and then have to avoid everyone who was present for at least a year in order to allow their memories to fade sufficiently. Being sober effectively eradicates the bullshit and leaves us with people who we really like in our lives.

There but for the Grace of God Go I – August 20th 2012

During the last week, I have experienced 'the darkness'

twice. It's enlightening, finding out a bit more about who I am (at the ripe old age of 36!) and not suffocating the bad emotions with too much wine; I am reaching a point close to acceptance of self. There is no perfection in humanity – all of our characters are flawed, but only now am I discovering all the facets of my personality in all their forms, giving them a chance to rise to the surface like lily-pads that have been weighted down on the bed of a stagnant pond.

I'll describe that dark place to you; it doesn't seem to arise for any particular reason but I know it's there from the minute I wake up. A dirty, blackened lens colours my view of everything that presents itself before me; the news on the TV is wrong, their take on a story is prejudiced, unfair. The clothes in my wardrobe are badly fitting, unfashionable, cheap-looking. My hair is frizzy and has no style. The weather is too hot or too cold. I haven't got enough money to do what I want to do, what would make me happy. Nobody understands me – the world is acting conspiratorially against me. My maternity leave is running out, time is moving too fast, and I don't want my baby to have to spend days away from me in a nursery. It makes me panic. The laundry is never-ending, the floor is perennially dirty. I'm fat; I can't shift the baby weight. I look like a middle-aged, tired mum in bad clothes. Make-up is fruitless, a waste of time. I can still see the lines and dark circles beneath my eyes. I am going grey. It builds and builds.

Before I stopped drinking, I would quash the panic with cold white wine. Its effect was instantaneous, washing away the bad thoughts and filling me up with a rosy glow, ameliorating the world in minutes. These days I go for a run.

On one of these self-medicating runs last week, I saw someone who shocked me to my core. This person is an ex-boyfriend from the days when I spent my life in self-destruct mode; a great catch and someone I think of often (not). In and out of prison for heroin-dealing, violent, a drug-dealer, an alcoholic fresh out of rehab for his smack problem, and who had found his Higher Power in Stella Artois and ecstasy pills, his redeeming features made an impressive list.

I had heard that he'd been seriously ill, that he'd been suffering from throat cancer and pneumonia, and that he'd been taking heroin again, but I hadn't seen him for ten years, so I wasn't prepared for what I saw. An old man of 46, shuffling along the pavement with a walking stick and a stooped back, shrivelled and weak and small. He had no charisma; his swagger had been annihilated by years of self-abuse. The man whom I used to walk into a pub with and watch as he bought three pints of Stella in one purchase (in order that he could down the first two like a runner drinking water at the end of a marathon before moving on to the third at a more relaxed pace) was no longer there. Never before has the expression 'a shadow of his former self' applied to a person so aptly. The man who used his bulk to push me around when I was twenty has almost succeeded in killing himself with drugs and drink, just sixteen years after our relationship ended.

I didn't speak to him. He didn't see me. His eyes were staring at the ground as he dragged his feet along, one in front of the other with slow deliberation. I couldn't take my eyes off him for a while. My black mood vanished without a trace. Oh, there but for the grace of God go I.

Things (not) to Do in Barcelona – August 22nd 2012

As a result of eating fewer cakes, drinking fewer lattes, and going for more runs, I have lost a total of about five pounds in as many weeks. Seems like a lot of sacrifice for a small reward, but at least the number is going in the right direction, and I am no longer dreading standing on the scales as I did in the final trimester of pregnancy. My weight during those last few months was increasing by about three or four pounds a week – I did wonder where it would end. Thankfully, I am fairly confident that I can wear my new (humongous on the chest coverage, due to breastfeeding boobs which resemble watermelons) bikini on the beach, without being fearful that Greenpeace might get called to drag me back into the water.

So we leave in four days for Mallorca; I have bought my miniature toiletries, new suitcase, and aforementioned monstrous bikini. The dog is booked in for kennels, the British summertime is winding down, and it looks like we will fly out of Manchester amidst pouring rain and chilly temperatures – always pleasing when you will depart at the other end of the flight straight in to thirty-five degrees and glorious sunshine.

And this holiday will, of course, be sans booze. There was a time when I couldn't imagine going away and not drinking, when I would almost not have seen the point of a holiday if it didn't include alcohol. And there were many holidays when booze was consumed on a nightly basis and good times were had by all, the wine adding to the general merriment and relaxed evenings that everyone wants from their week in the sun. But in the last few years there were many times when I drank not to be sociable and fun and relaxed, but to get hammered; when I drank alcoholically.

Example; Barcelona, the Ramblas, circa 2004. My travel companion and I hit the beers mid-afternoon, and continued to sink many *cerveza de pequeñas* in thirty-five degree heat (not really relevant – if it had been minus ten, we would still have got as wasted as we did. I'm using the temperature as a bit of an excuse here) well into the night. My memory is a little cloudy but I remember sitting in a plaza, people-watching, and downing my third or fourth drink. Time then becomes fluid; snippets of conversations flicker through my mind but vast gaps emerge, leaving me with a staccato recollection of the latter part of the evening.

An argument sprang up between us (there is a theme here, me + boyfriend + alcohol = massive fight) which led to two members of *La Policia* intervening in what they thought was a domestic violence matter (I was acting like a melodramatic idiot, and my boyfriend was holding on to me while he attempted to calm me down; this was construed as him assaulting me). After a lengthy altercation between the four of us in downtown Barcelona, we were allowed to leave and scarpered back to our hotel, him muttering about my inability to hold my drink, me blaming him for attracting the attention of the police. It was messy, embarrassing. We fell in to liquor-induced comas upon reaching our hotel bedroom, approximately three hours before we had to be up for the journey home.

Plane departure time; 0800 hours. Time we awoke; 0700 hours. Panic. We grabbed the clothes that were strewn around the room, bundled them in to our cases, and ran downstairs to check out. Somewhere amidst the previous evening's activities, the strap across the top of my Birkenstock sandal had come unstuck, leaving me with a shoe-shaped piece of cork and a flap of white leather as one half of my footwear. In my hungover state of mind this troubled me, so much so that as we raced through Barcelona airport with minus five minutes before take-off, I discarded the sad-looking sandals in to a rubbish bin and veered in to a shoe shop in order to purchase a more respectable-looking pair. Oh, the joy on my boyfriend's face! Boarding the plane fifteen minutes post-departure time, we received the obligatory round of applause that passengers award to the crap, hungover people who almost miss their flight due to over-refreshing themselves the previous evening.

This holiday will be sans booze, sans drunken arguments, sans broken sandals. There will be no fracas with the local constabulary, no almost-missed flights. There will, however, be relaxing afternoons spent by the pool, bowlfuls of *patatas bravas*, our baby's first swim, browsing in dark, Mallorcan shops for souvenirs, and a photo album's worth of happy holiday pictures for my family to return to time and time again. I can't wait.

Reasons Why I Drank – August 24th 2012

I started drinking heavily in my mid-teens and continued to do so until I hit 35. I often think about the factors that led me to drink alcoholically, because I know it was more than simply sustained exposure. Right from the off I drank to get drunk and I never, ever got it when people professed to sipping a single glass of wine with dinner or to 'blowing the froth off a couple' on the way home from work. When I poured the first glass of the night, it was with one intention in mind; to down as much booze as I could get away with before I either a) passed out or b) ran out of alcohol, whichever came first.

People often said to me that I was lacking in some kind of inherent off-switch, a magic voice that I consistently saw manifest itself in others and for which I longingly craved, a voice that would tell me to stop when I had had enough; a watchful guardian in my head, persuading me to go home while I could still stand.

I have always been a funny bugger in that I am most definitely an introverted extrovert, or an extroverted introvert, or some such contradiction. Shy on the outside with a lot going on inside and an obstacle sandwiched between the two, preventing the voice inside from being heard. Reason number one why I drank – I am actually a little bit shy, and often struggle to have conversations with people who I don't know very well. Thus the discovery of the following equation was (for a long while) the key to social success; shy girl + wine = chatty and fun girl. Over time, the equation morphed into this; shy girl + wine = annoying twat.

Early on in my teens I developed a rabid interest in the opposite sex. I don't recall ever being struck with a debilitating shyness around boys, but I do know that once I threw some alcohol into the mix the dating game became a whole lot easier. So, reason number two: being sexy and intoxicating to the male of the species becomes easy as pie when you have knocked back a bottle of wine. Ditto the above; over time, shy girl + wine = annoying twat of a girlfriend.

I get bored very easily. I often feel as though life is just slipping through my fingers like sand, and I am overwhelmed by a desire to make it all the cream. I don't do banal very well. Alcohol injects fun, although now I see that this was really an illusion. When I drank, I thought that those nights when everyone lets their hair down and bonds over meaningless conversations, and quiet nights at home transformed after a few bottles have been drunk during discos in the living room, were real. I imagined that the closeness and friendships forged through inebriation would last, and that they meant something.

On many nights I would find myself waking up in the early hours in a strange bed in the dark of a spare room, where someone had carried me because I had got drunk and embarrassing. Until the penny dropped there was reason number three: get drunk and life gets more fun. Reason number four was to drown out the darkness, to forget my worries, number five: to mask loneliness. And number six, the most stupid of all, to sufficiently wipe away the self-hatred and shame that coursed through every inch of me, owing to the vast amount of alcohol I had consumed the night before.

And the truth is that every feeling I tried to create, every social interaction I tried to lubricate, and every personality trait that I tried to fake, has blown away like a puff of smoke now that the glass is empty. Whatever life you think is yours amidst an alcohol-fuelled existence will be nothing more than a hazy recollection of falseness in sobriety.

Letter to Me, Aged 14 – September 6th 2012

You are full of confidence and assertiveness, passion and motivation. You know exactly who you are and where you are going; there isn't a doubt in your mind that life is bountiful and yours for the taking. You've got friends you value, there always seems to be a boy in the background, and you work reasonably hard at school, although luckily you manage to coast through anyway without too much effort. Life is a breeze.

Next week you are going to get drunk. Your friend's parents are away on holiday and together you will raid the spirits supply in the antique wooden cabinet in the lounge. There will be a couple of boys there and you will all think that you are so grown-up and sophisticated, even at the tender age of fourteen. As your body begins to absorb the alcohol, you will feel a surge of adrenaline and a sudden confidence boost. You will flirt a little more than you would've done ordinarily, you'll become boisterous and slightly aggressive towards your friend. She will come to the conclusion that you are someone to be wary of; your sudden mood change will frighten her, and over the course of the next few weeks you will drift apart.

You will begin to socialise with other people who enjoy getting drunk and you will continue to spend your weekends drinking until you knock yourself out. It won't be a passing fancy, all this booze. Without realising it, you will get sucked into a trap and it will take over twenty years before you realise what's happened and you finally find the strength to escape.

In that time you will get married and have a baby who

you will love more than anything you have ever loved before, and without whom you would no doubt have sunk lower and lower into the mire that you will find yourself in. You will get divorced and this will push you over the edge, forcing you through a rickety barrier that was keeping you from falling too far. You won't understand how your marriage failed, and your ex-husband will do nothing to help build a solid foundation on which you can base your separated family upon. He won't even tell you why he left.

This is the worst time – if only you could see then what I can see now, and put down the bottle. But you really feel as though you need it, that life has become so painful that you can't get through the night without it, that you can't stop yourself from falling to pieces completely unless you numb the agony with more and more alcohol. You carry on, unaware that, as you pinball between awful situations, it's the booze that's creating the longevity of the pain.

You will maintain a certain status quo. Most importantly you will keep your daughter's life on an even keel and, for the most part, you will keep your drinking hidden from her. You will hold down jobs and have your own house, but you will always be hitting way below your potential during these years. You keep your head above water but only just, and you could have done so much more with your time.

But after several years, thoughts stir in your mind; you will begin to wonder if you are out of control with regard to the alcohol you consume, and you will start to walk down a path that will eventually lead you to sobriety. When you are thirty-five, you will meet someone whom you wished that you'd met years ago. This man will motivate you to stop drinking and help you believe that you are far better than you ever thought you were. You will have a beautiful baby girl with him, and this time you will act differently.

Because you've left the booze behind, you'll have more energy and patience, you will be kinder and more thoughtful. You will throw everything that you can at building a happy life for yourself and your family. You will understand that alcohol robbed you of many things but you won't feel sorry for yourself because of it. You will use your experiences to try and help other people see what you know to be true; that there is nothing to be gained from drinking, and everything to be had from living your life clean and well, without addiction.

Knocking it on the Head – September 10th 2012

When I first emerged from the wreck that my alcohol dependency had created, I felt battered and small – my personality had been manipulated and shaped by addiction and shame for so long that I no longer knew who I was. I'm not sure if, in the first few weeks, I truly believed that I would never drink again. There was an element of self-doubt that teased my newly sober self with the thought that I couldn't do it, that over time I would forget the horror of my last encounter with booze and I would cave in and begin to drink again. But I stopped drinking for a sufficiently long period to allow myself the first taste of being me without the prop of alcohol, and during that time I recognised and learnt things about myself and my relationship with booze that cemented my commitment to teetotalism. A major step forward was to admit to myself that I had a dependency upon alcohol.

The UK Alcoholics Anonymous website states that while they do not offer a formal definition of alcoholism, the majority of their members would agree on the following statement; "... it could be described as a physical compulsion, coupled with a mental obsession. What we mean is that we had a distinct physical desire to consume alcohol beyond our capacity to control it, in defiance of all rules of common sense. We not only had an abnormal craving for alcohol but we frequently yielded to it at the worst possible times. We did not know when (or how) to stop drinking. Often we did not seem to have sense enough to know when not to begin."

This description fits perfectly with my relationship with alcohol, but it took several weeks of being sober for me to recognise that I was an alcohol addict. As soon as I took a sip from my first drink my mind would begin to whir frenetically, as it attempted to map out the most effective way to consume as much booze as possible before someone intervened and told me I'd had too much. This was the reason why drinking alone was always so much more enjoyable for me – there was never a killjoy leaping forward to impose his or her own restrictive behaviour on me when all I wanted to do was get hammered.

And so, armed with this newfound awareness, I slowly accepted that I was dependent upon alcohol and therefore I had a responsibility to those around me and to myself to stop for good. No single factor would have been sufficient in prompting me to get on top of my problematic relationship with booze – rather, elements in my life began to come together like a jigsaw puzzle which, once complete, presented something of a eureka moment to me. The years of destructive and shameful behaviour and the associated self-hatred and a growing sense of mortality that grew at the same rate that my youthful ignorance of personal responsibility diminished, meeting my fiancé and developing an awareness of who I really was without the façade of drinking – it was all of these things that pushed me into that place where I had wanted and needed to get for so many years.

And now, here I am – seventeen months of sobriety and what feels like a lifetime of self-discovery later; a much calmer, honest, more confident woman who is enjoying a normal existence after twenty-one years of self-abuse.

I knew that I had come on leaps and bounds when on

holiday last week, as I didn't miss alcohol one bit. Conversely, if someone had put a bottle of pinot in front of me and told me that I could drink it with none of the associated negativity, without the hangover or the guilt or the damage to my health, I would have happily walked away and not touched a drop.

Silent Voices – September 11th 2012

The Children's Commissioner, Dr Maggie Atkinson, has today published a report entitled 'Silent Voices' which highlights the impact of alcohol misuse on children.[2] The report was commissioned owing to a growing concern about the number of children in the UK who currently live with parents who regularly binge drink, and the effect that this has on their emotional wellbeing and development. The report suggests that one in three children in the UK lives with at least one parent who regularly binge drinks, and that there are approximately 460,000 children living with a single parent who regularly binge drinks.

Up until seventeen months ago, my elder daughter (now almost fourteen) was one of those children. Before she reached the age of about eight or nine, I generally managed to keep my drinking hidden from her. She has always been a fantastic sleeper and so once she had gone to bed I would hit the wine, safe in the knowledge that she most likely wouldn't come downstairs. As she grew older, there were occasions when she stayed up later (New Year's Eve, Christmas, birthday celebrations, holidays, for instance) and then she did witness my excessive drinking. I am ashamed to say that she saw me drunk several times.

More disturbing for her, I think, were the countless

---

[2] www.childrenscommissioner.gov.uk/content/publications/content_620

days when I had the mother of all hangovers and I would stomp about the house like a bear with a sore head, snapping at her for the tiniest of reasons. I couldn't be bothered to read her letters from school properly, or help her with her homework, or go swimming with her, or take her to the park. My head would be throbbing and my energy levels so depleted by the alcohol that it was all I could do to drag myself out of bed and sit in front of mindless TV with her.

Don't get me wrong, there were times when I did act like a proper mummy and devote myself and my time to my wonderful little girl, but there were many times when I did not. The hungover days began to be the norm in the last few years, and my daughter's perception of me was one of a miserable old grump who was no fun at all. This insidious side-effect of regular binge drinking has a very real and detrimental effect upon the children of binge drinkers.

The Silent Voices report, I hope, will make the government sit up and notice how damaging binge drinking is in this country, and perhaps spur them on to doing something a little more helpful than creating the 'Responsibility Deal', introduced in the summer of 2010 in an effort to tackle the country's growing drinking problem, and which appears to have been reduced to little more than a series of half-baked undertakings. If parents were regularly binging on class A drugs in the same numbers as those who partake in alcohol abuse, the House of Commons would be in uproar. As alcohol is legal, and enjoyed by the majority of government ministers, concern is rather more tempered.

Parents should read this report and question whether their drinking impacts on their children. If one in three children are living with at least one binge drinker, then the effect on the next generation could be tremendous. Both my daughters now enjoy a mum who is happy and energetic and full of life, which is what every child deserves to have.

The Circle of Life – September 14th 2012

I don't know whether the thoughts I have been having latterly about life are as a result of a) having a baby recently, b) giving up drinking recently or c) growing older recently.[3]

I wrote in an earlier post (**Robert the Geranium Plant**) that in my view you don't grow as a person when you regularly get wasted, drinking to obliterate happiness and sadness and emptiness and joyfulness and loneliness. You only develop your character when you face everything that life hurls at you, head on. You can't protect yourself by hiding behind the flimsy shield of booze; in doing so, you are essentially freezing your emotional maturity, and the day will come when life will demand a level of sensibility of you and you just won't be able to cut the mustard.

Anyway, today my thoughts turned to the circle of life. As I fed my baby, I realised that this precious life in my arms, the responsibility that I have for her life, isn't simply for the living, breathing physical being that I was holding. It is for everything that should be hers during the next seventy or eighty years, or for however long she will live for on this earth. The life that sleeps in a cot as I write this is an education, a graduation, a first kiss, friendships, nights out with friends, nights in alone, tears of happiness and of sadness, grieving, celebrations, a marriage, giving

---

[3] I understand that we are all growing older from the day we are born and therefore this can't be a thing you do recently, or something that you used to do – it is something that you do, always. But I mean growing older in a different sense; I mean growing in wisdom.

birth, wondering what to wear, being on a diet, feeling fantastic, having a bad hair day, walking a dog, flying a kite, achieving goals, fulfilling a dream, enjoying a good book, learning a language, passing a driving test, getting a parking ticket, grazing a knee, doing the shopping, falling in love, breaking up, getting a promotion, developing a crush. That is the weight of the responsibility of having a child – the life that you create is the decades on this earth. It is living, in its entirety.

Later, as I pushed the pram through the park, Lily gazing upwards at the leaves wafting on the trees, I passed a trio of old ladies drinking tea outside the café. And when I looked at them, I saw their lives. I didn't see old ladies at a standstill in time, grey and wrinkled, forever stuck in a state of decrepitude as if they had been born that way and would always be that way. I saw a fluctuating motion of lives being lived, a recognition that we are all in infancy and childhood, youth and middle-age, grey and dying. We cannot be characterised by age when we are all moving through life in one perpetual process of growing older. Those ladies were not frozen in time, their proximity to the end static with their deaths arriving like a sudden shock, a bolt out of the blue that nobody saw coming. Those ladies represented life.

At one time they were celebrating their weddings, holding their newborn babies, choosing a dress for a special occasion, getting frustrated in a traffic jam, soothing a poorly child, dropping the children off at school, passing exams, going for a job interview, losing a loved one, making a cake, going to work. The ladies drinking tea were once the baby in someone's arms, and the only difference between them and Lily is that they have had most of their time on earth already.

So, there I was, pondering these thoughts and ambling along, and thinking that in all the time I drank alcohol, I never thought things like this. And I asked myself, am I experiencing this moment of clarity as a result of a) having a baby recently, b) giving up drinking recently, or c) growing older recently?

Probably a combination of all three.

"Five years from now, you're the same person except for the people you've met and the books you've read." – John Wooden, October 14th 1910 – September 18th 2012

Aged 17 – October 14, 1992

You are living in the moment, never looking further than the next weekend, drifting further into the nightclub scene. You are a raver, dressed in your catsuit and trainers; hair sleek in a bob, lips red, newly aware of your femininity. Music is everything, the underground scene is hypnotic; its naughtiness and illegality is like a drug, club fliers adorn your bedroom wall replacing your posters of The Smiths and Depeche Mode. First year of A-levels but you've outgrown it now, it's a burden on your time. Life flows eternally before you, there are no worries and no cares other than a strange persuasion you have developed to almost enjoy the dark side, to wallow in your suffering and to emulate your heroine, Laura Palmer of Twin Peaks – a strange one to pick given her untimely death, preceded by a life afflicted by drug addiction and abuse.

Aged 22 – October 14, 1997

Oh, you emulated Laura all right, other than her murder – and that isn't such an unlikely possibility these days. A recreational enjoyment of clubs and their associated pleasures has strayed into the murky waters of grim addiction; the only friends you have are in the same boat. Thrown out of a nightclub on this, your birthday, for being so out of it; you aren't demonstrating an ounce of care for your safety, and you don't eat much at all. Your hair is short, your body is thin; you virtually live in a pub exclusively frequented by abusers of alcohol and drugs. You're going down, down, down …

Aged 27 – October 14, 2002

Dragged out of the sinking sand by the arrival of your gorgeous baby girl, she is now three years old and the apple of your eye. Her dad, your husband, is busy working all the hours God sends – mostly you spend time with your friends. When your baby is in bed, you drink; it's not so much, a few bottles of beer or a bottle of wine with a meal, and at the weekend it's more. There are parties and nights out with girlfriends, where drinking is the thing to do, drinking enough to occasionally act in a way you regret. But the regrets are few and far between, life is for the living, mortality is a concept that, so far, you don't acknowledge. One year left of your degree – studying is time well spent, an effort to establish a foundation on which to someday build a career. That day might come sooner than you think, because your marriage is almost done.

Aged 32 – October 14, 2007

Ooh, happy birthday you! Four years since the breakdown of your marriage, things are no longer so pretty. Wine is a staple of your existence – it tends to your every emotion; happy, sad, bored, depressed, lonely … drinking in company is getting harder – the necessary control over the amount you consume is a struggle. Your self-esteem has taken a battering, over and over again there's an action that you regret or words you wished had been left unsaid. Your office job bores you to tears, there should be more to life than this – drinking is an aid to forgetting. Relationships are hard to sustain, difficult to work out. Being a mother keeps your head out of the water, but the current is strong and it's dragging you down.

Aged 37 – October 14, 2012

Just under four weeks from now, I will turn 37. On numerous occasions during my life, I've wondered whether I would live as long as this. Many times my thoughts turned to suicide; I never fully grasped the notion as a plan of action, but the tendency to ponder whether life should ever be this arduous, this painful, was ever present for a long time. My little girl consistently provided the reason why life is always worth it, no matter how tough things became, and for that (as well as for a myriad of other reasons) I am eternally grateful that I have her in my world. She saved me.

As every five-yearly interval in my life passed, things didn't seem to change direction much. I was sitting in a boat, adrift in an ocean of depression and misunderstanding of what life is about, carried along on a current of self-destruction and pity, never looking far enough into the distance to seek out another way. That is, until a couple of years ago.

This last five-year interval represents a series of events that have gently prodded and pulled me this way and that, tugging me into a place that is warm and happy and safe. It's a place I never thought I'd find myself in – where the walls of depression and self-hatred have crumbled away to leave an open space, full of endless possibilities. It's the place where I've found my soul mate, had my second daughter, and truly arrived at the realisation of what my life should be. I never want to leave this place behind.

The Only Thing to Fear Is Fear Itself – September 21st 2012

Now that I have been sober for about a year and a half and I love my life without the alcohol-related sluggishness, lack of productivity, grumpiness, mood swings, bad complexion, and much-reduced finances, I sometimes look back on the twenty years that I spent mostly getting drunk and wonder why the hell it took me so long to put a cork in it.

Ten years prior to me becoming teetotal I had an inkling that I was drinking too much, that my relationship with alcohol was unhealthy. There were many occasions when I got utterly smashed, waking up with no memory of the previous night or (sometimes) worse, only bits and pieces of memory that linked together an evening littered with embarrassing actions and regretful words that I mostly wished I hadn't remembered.

Five years prior to quitting, the fear set in. Often at night, when I hadn't slipped into an alcohol-induced coma, I would lie awake in the dark touching my chest, checking for lumps. I became paranoid that I had breast cancer as a result of my awful lifestyle – smoking and drinking to excess, eating rubbish, not eating enough. My consciousness was riddled with fear. Night after night I tormented myself that my mortality would be realised sooner than it ought to be. I read voraciously articles about binge drinking, alcoholism, drug addiction, depression. I was acutely aware of the statistical evidence relating to women binge drinkers and the associated increase in liver disease and cancers, and yet I did not attempt to sober up.

The reason that I did not seek help is because I was frightened. I was frightened of walking into a room full of strangers and saying that I was an alcoholic. I was frightened that I had inflicted irreversible liver damage on myself, or that upon seeking help a doctor might discover any one of a plethora of horrendous diseases, festering undeterred in my body. I was frightened that if I stopped drinking alcohol I would be forced to endure the rest of my days gagging for wine, salivating each time I walked past a beer garden on a hot summer's day, drooling whenever I ate a meal in a restaurant surrounded by bottles of wine being glugged appreciatively by other diners. And because I was so frightened, I continued to drink. And drink, and drink.

Finally I made the decision to quit drinking because of that night back in April 2011. The bottom dropped out of my world in the small hours of the morning after, and when I regained my senses I came to the conclusion, at last, that I never wanted to touch alcohol again. Despite knowing in my heart that my rollercoaster ride with booze was over for ever, I still held on to the fear that I had lost my best friend – my companion, shoulder to cry on, ego-booster, courage-giver, and the one who could always be relied upon to inject fun into any situation.

In the immediate aftermath I often questioned my dependency, for (as anyone who makes the decision to leave alcohol behind will tell you) the issue of self-diagnosis is a thorny one. You wonder how you can be an alcohol addict when those around you are getting out of their heads every weekend; why nice people in films get wasted together and the audience don't find their characters repellent; why family celebrations are a hotbed of drunkenness and nobody seems to care. Why are you an alcoholic and they are just enjoying a drink? Where is the line? Who draws the line?

The answers to those questions are not easy, but the further removed I become from an existence sullied by alcohol abuse, the more I appreciate how much better life is since I gave myself a chance to be me, minus the mask.

Plant, Pet, then Person – September 22nd 2012

Years ago I had a friend who was in therapy. She told me that her therapist had given her the following advice; first, get a plant. When you can keep it alive and thriving for more than six months, get yourself a pet. If you can maintain its health and happiness and nobody reports you to the RSPCA for abandonment or worse, then think about having a relationship with a human being.

I wish I had taken notice of this when my marriage broke up. My husband and I had kept a few pot plants in the house, and one by one they withered and died as I nursed my shattered soul over too much wine, immersing myself in a pool of misery which was akin to swimming through mud for the first few months. There wasn't much room for being green-fingered. At the same time, I was attempting to look after our dog, Mowgli, and here is a story in itself.

My ex-husband walked out on me and my little girl when she was just four, on Valentine's Day and the day after I had fallen down the stairs (not drunk for once in my life!) and broken my foot, causing an impressive metatarsal shatter that was similar to one David Beckham had around the time (or so I was excitedly told by the football-fanatic doctor who X-rayed me).

We had acquired a puppy just six months previously, a wonderful ball of energy that was so extraordinarily full of love and joy while simultaneously being utterly devoid of sense, the ability to be trained, and even the merest hint of a brain. Given the timing of the marriage split (February), the roads were covered in sheet ice, snow lay around in piles of exhaust-fume blackened sludge, and temperatures were not particularly kind.

The dog had boundless energy and could have easily handled a couple of ten mile walks in the morning, followed by a quick swim across the English Channel and back again in time for his kibble. My daughter was small and had short four-year-old's legs and not the slightest inclination to walk further than to the corner shop and back for sweets. I had a plaster cast on my leg and was on crutches. You might say we were in something of a pickle.

We muddled by though, gratefully accepting the help of wonderful friends and family, taking the dog out wherever possible and throwing balls for him in the field at the bottom of the road in order to tire him out, and trying to remain sanguine when he ate our coats and shoes. I would bite my lip and fight back the tears when I routinely hobbled home on my crutches to find yet another piece of expensive furniture that he had ripped apart in a fit of pique at being left on his own for longer than half an hour.

One time, he managed to open the kitchen cupboard under the sink and pull out its entire contents. Scores of plastic bags were shredded and strewn around the floor, intermingled with two supersize sacks' worth of dog kibble which he had opened with his teeth, bottles of detergents and washing up liquid had been chewed and spilt all over the wooden floor, mixing with the other debris to create a sloppy, slippery, horrendous mess that took me hours to clean up.

After six months, I gave the dog to a re-homing place nearby. He was only one year old, and I knew that if a dog lover, with more time and energy on his hands than I had at the time, took him on, he would be able to build him up to become a fine adult dog. He just needed patience and time and lots of long walks – three things that I was not able to provide him with at the time. After parting with my beloved puppy, I should have taken the hint; relationships with humans were never going to work for me while I was in that place. I had such a longing, however, to rebuild my family, to find a replacement dad for the one who had buggered off with somebody else that I wasn't as discerning as I might have been in my choice of boyfriends.

I remember at the time simply craving a family unit, and it coloured my vision. With hindsight I should have just waited until Mr Right (who is currently asleep upstairs) came along and swept me off in a cloud of happiness. Could have, would have, should have.

And I hope, Mowgli, that, wherever you found yourself, you had a happy life and understood that we loved you so much. I really, truly, wish that I had kept you and rebuffed humans (in the boyfriend sense) for a while. I wish I could have made you into the dog that you should have been.

I'm sorry.

Have You Got a Drinking Problem? – September 28th 2012

I was talking to a journalist yesterday about the Soberistas project and she asked me the following question; "What is the difference between the way you used to drink, and the way I drink (i.e. having a gin and tonic in the evening to relax – just the one, drinking responsibly)?"

I told her that when I used to drink I never opened a bottle of wine without knowing that I would finish it, I always did a recce upon arriving at an event in order to establish how much booze would be made available to me, and the phrase 'drinking responsibly' – well, that was left wide open to my interpretation. I engaged in a lot of denial back then and I had a few tricks up my addict's sleeve which I called upon to cushion the knowledge that my alcohol intake had reached epic proportions.

Drinking responsibly was something that middle-class people did. If I bought my wine from Waitrose and it was a ten-quid bottle of chablis or a twenty-quid bottle of barolo, that was drinking responsibly. Forget the fact that I drank two or three of them, amounting to roughly three times my weekly safe limit in one night. When I carefully placed my rinsed bottles in my Heals' recycling bin, I was drinking responsibly. Dropping those bottles off at the Waitrose recycling bin was drinking responsibly. Meeting friends for a glass of fizz in the nice Italian bar down the road, sitting outside in the sun all dressed up and feeling sophisticated, that was drinking responsibly. And drinking a juicy Rioja with a steaming bowl of pasta, candlelit table, romance all around – that was drinking responsibly.

Human powers of denial are tenacious, as was my inability to recognise that booze, dressed up in whichever way, is still booze. With each tenner I spent in Waitrose's wine section (can I just point out that I love Waitrose and John Lewis, really I do. Definitely my supermarket/ department store of choice – this is purely to illustrate my point that I was truly gifted at kidding myself for a fifth of a century with regards to my alcohol addiction), I was slowly poisoning myself.

Further to my point that I love the John Lewis partnership, I do still enjoy parting with my money in their stores, but now it goes on food, perfume, nice vases, cushions, lovely clothes, and pleasing bath products.

Anyway – is your drinking problematic? Are you a responsible drinker or an irresponsible drinker? As an aside, when you Google the word 'responsibly', the top suggestions that appear are 'beer', 'vodka' and 'brewery' … Interesting.

Say Goodbye to the Muffin Top – October 6th 2012

What a difference a day makes. I've spent the last couple of days feeling pretty flat with regards to keeping fit (I just wrote fat there by mistake – how telling!) and shifting this last stone of baby weight. I signed up for a 10k race which takes place on December 2nd and I am starting to worry slightly that I may not be able to complete it, never mind improve on my Personal Best (which was achieved approximately 10 years ago). None of this was making me feel particularly positive. Oh yes, to disconcert the healthy-lifestyle apple cart further, I seem to have gradually upped my biscuit and chocolate munching once again – this week it's been close to the epic pregnancy portions, which is never going to make me happy. Or thin.

But this morning as I lay in bed at 6 a.m. with Lily gurgling next to me, I began to think about willpower and positive mental attitude – how I have managed to successfully transform myself from binge-drinking, manic depressive, bipolar-esque boozer, to calm, happy, level-headed person who is much nicer to be around (I hope). I didn't switch from one persona to the other by accident, or with no effort. I did it by altering my state of mind.

Prior to giving up alcohol for good, I regularly knocked it on the head for short periods of, say, six weeks or three months. I would spend the entire duration of my wagon rides miserable as sin, drooling whenever I thought of wine. At the end of these aeons of alcohol deprivation, my spirits would lift once again as I embarked on a good old piss-up by way of a reward for my abstinence. I'd give myself a good pat on the back too for not being an alcoholic – after all, if I could manage six weeks without booze then surely I couldn't be dependent upon the stuff?

In order to stop drinking for good and to be happy about it, I had to alter my thought processes. Without alcohol in my life, I wasn't depriving myself of something desirable; I was giving myself the benefits of good health, happier state of mind and improved physical appearance. Without alcohol, I am able to go running whenever I want, I don't have to worry about what I said or did the night before – ever (that is so freeing), I never suffer from a furry tongue, bad breath, or dried leather-handbag skin owing to dehydration, I have more money, my fears about dying prematurely have vanished, I no longer have panic attacks, my self-confidence has improved massively, I have tons more energy, and I don't hate myself. Looking over that list makes me wonder why the hell I ever drank in the first place!

So, back to my ponderings this morning – in order to get back in pre-pregnancy shape, I need to apply the same state-of-mind-alteration to my cake-munching and fitness programme. I read an article yesterday about Alzheimer's now being regarded as Type-2 diabetes, in that recent research suggests that it is brought on by eating too many sugary and processed foods. Cakes and biscuits are bad for us; they keep us from reaching our desired weight loss goals, they're bad for our teeth, they provide absolutely no nutritional benefit whatsoever, and they cost money that could be spent on better things. Now they may even be responsible for the onset of Alzheimer's disease. I want to lose a stone and I want to be able to run a good time when I take part in the 10k in December. Cakes ain't gonna help me do either.

So, with cakes out of the window and a new, more positive state of mind in place, I did 100 crunches followed by a one-minute plank this morning in my PJs, and I am going to take the dog for a five-mile run shortly. I skipped my usual cake at the café and I am planning on repeating my crunches/plank regime every day. Incidentally I have never followed a fitness regime for any length of time that specifically targets one area of the body, so I am intrigued to see how effective this will be. I am feeling much happier as a result of this mind change – it's good to discover yet another positive from giving up the booze, which is that if I can get that shit out of my life then I can pretty much achieve anything I want – happy days! (I'll keep you posted re the six-pack).

Under the Bridge – October 8th 2012

This morning as I drove my eldest daughter to school, we had our usual spat over which radio station to put on (she likes Capital – urrghh – and I favour Radio 2). We've been having the same semi-serious argument on the school run for approximately a year now, ever since she grew old enough to stop listening solely to the music that I, so devotedly, brought her up on. I think back fondly to the halcyon days when she had the Red Hot Chili Peppers, Nirvana, and Blondie on her iPod, whereas now she is all over Ne-Yo, Rita Ora and Nicki Minaj and has developed an irritating habit of dissing my music choices (should I ever be lucky enough to get something of my choice played).

As we drove along, she singing merrily to some R&B drivel and me gritting my teeth and telling myself that in just another few minutes I would be able to switch over to Chris Evans and the interminable noise I was being subjected to would stop, I caught hold of myself and had a quick reconfiguration of my thoughts. Isn't it the law that all parents hate their teenage children's music? And that when those teenage children are parents, they still think that the music they listened to as a kid is brilliant?

Example: Haddaway, 'What is Love?' I love that song. When I hear it I am instantly transported to a nightclub in Greece – me aged nineteen dancing on top of a podium (hmm, yes, really) and wearing a very small top, tight hipster shorts, and boots. Even at 8:30 a.m. returning home from the school run, if that song comes on the radio, the volume gets cranked up and I am a happy bunny. It changes my mindset for the better and makes me feel young again.

In my darkest drinking days, I was ridiculously obsessed with the Red Hot Chili Peppers. I still love them, but back then I was annoyingly infatuated with them. I have lost track of the number of times I watched 'Live at Slane Castle', bottle of pinot to hand (or three), losing myself in Anthony Kiedis and his wonderful, bizarre dancing. I fell in love exceptionally hard with RHCP owing to their lyrics about addiction (albeit their demon was heroin, mine was a nice chablis or pinot grigio from Waitrose).

'Under the Bridge' was, for me, not so much about shooting up in downtown LA with a bunch of Mexican rude boys as lying on the settee with a cut-crystal glass full to the brim with wine, *Sex and the City* on the TV and a copy of *OK!* magazine on the coffee table. 'Otherside' provided me with a way to get over the self-hatred I used to feel the morning after excessive amounts of booze the night before, the sense of desperation in the song being utterly relevant to where I found myself mentally most weekends.

I have always loved many different types of music, but pretty much all of it is from either when I was growing up or when I was struggling mentally. There's the odd current song that I hear on the radio that becomes a new favourite, but it's rare. I am emotionally attached to the music of my youth, and from later on in my life, from the days I spent struggling with depression and the abuse of alcohol.

I gave myself a silent smack on the wrist this morning and bit my lip when I felt the urge to shout "What's this rubbish? Who the hell is Nicki Minaj anyway??" Instead, I drove along in silence, focusing on the thoughts I have written about above. It is my darling daughter's God-given right to love music that I hate. It's what she should be doing. And when she is in her 30s and 40s, her kids will be telling her that Rita Ora is rubbish, and that she should get with it and start listening to whatever claptrap they are fixated on. At least, I hope they will.

Hitting the Bottle – October 13th 2012

As my baby is almost six months old, I have made the decision to stop breastfeeding. Yesterday I reduced the breastfeeds down to just one at bed time and plan to gradually decrease these over the coming week. A catalyst for this is because tomorrow I turn thirty-seven and my other half, my eldest daughter, and I are off to 'Go Ape.' Here we will spend a few hours swinging around tree tops and whizzing down zip wires; my alternative plan to the usual 'let's get plastered in a pub somewhere' notion of how to have fun on your birthday (zip wiring was suggested by Sue of Soberistas – thank you Sue). Mum and Dad are baby-sitting hence it seems as good a time as any to begin the switch to bottle-feeding.

Giving up breastfeeding is an emotional rollercoaster – for me at least. I will most likely not have another baby and so it follows that I will never breastfeed again once I finish for good in a few days. There is something so uniquely wonderful about nursing your child, having the knowledge that you are providing her only sustenance and sharing a bond that no other person on the planet could have with your baby. Those middle-of-the-night rendezvous, the two of you cuddled together in private harmony, innately understanding just what it is you are meant to be doing to keep the other happy, the gulf of age bridged by the simple act of supplying food – there is nothing like it in the world. And I know that I will miss it.

I am happy that I chose to feed my baby in this way for the first half-year of her life, and I am even happier that the reason I am now switching to bottles is not because I want to drink alcohol again. I breastfed my eldest child for sixteen weeks, and at the age of twenty-three that felt like an eternity. Keen to get out socialising again (for socialising, read 'boozing') I knocked the nursing on the head in favour of being able to get drunk with my friends again.

I realise that age brings wisdom, but it still fills me with sadness that I could not recognise what a wonderful privilege breastfeeding is, and how making the 'sacrifice' of being teetotal for a further six months post-pregnancy is no sacrifice at all when you are providing your baby with such a good start in life. (I know that some mothers are unable to breastfeed, and their children are perfectly healthy – I don't mean to point the finger here. It worked for me, and so I am naturally in its favour).

My life is becoming busier and I am working a lot on our upcoming website, Soberistas.com, therefore becoming more reliant on other people babysitting Lily. I have also fulfilled what I set out to do – exclusive breastfeeding for the first six months (just shy by a week or two). And yet deciding to switch to bottles marks a new chapter for my baby; that magical, primal connection that the two of us have enjoyed since the day I discovered I was pregnant is reaching its conclusion. It feels like she is embarking upon the first tiny step she will take towards independence.

When I finished breastfeeding my eldest daughter, I remember being overwhelmed with guilt and confusion, but I went ahead and did it anyway. I knew that the real reason behind me switching her to bottles was because I hankered after getting some of my old life back, I felt as though I had done 'my bit' to a degree and I just wanted to get on with living. There are none of those feelings this time around, just an acceptance that now seems like the right time, for me and the baby, and the knowledge that I will miss it (although the thought of getting a proper night's sleep is wonderful!) once it has gone.

When I feed her for the last time, it will be an emotional experience. But again I am reminded of how much I have grown up and become less selfish as a result of quitting drinking alcohol – I have made a measured decision, weighing up the pros and cons for both of us (mainly the baby) and doing what is right for her, primarily. I will continue to be teetotal, to eat nutritious food (and now to begin cooking/pureeing it for the baby too) and to treat my body with respect, just as I had to do during pregnancy and breastfeeding. I will do all that because I finally have some self-respect, it makes me happy and because I am setting an example to my two girls.

Go Ape! – October 16th 2012

I can count on one hand the times in my life when I have been truly terrified. There were the births of both my daughters; I hold my hand up and admit that, despite voraciously soaking up as much knowledge about hypnobirthing, water births, and earth mothers chilling with a brew minutes after popping their little one out, I was utterly terrified about the whole experience from about six months pregnant onwards. The actual events did nothing to put my fears into perspective, I may add.

There was the time when I found myself in a tricky situation with a violent ex-boyfriend who decided that he wasn't too chuffed about me dumping him and took it upon himself to break into the house I was staying in and telling me, with the aid of a hammer, exactly what he thought of me.

Then there was the skydive that I did a few years ago when, despite me fooling myself and anyone who would listen that I was a crazy, extreme sports fanatic who just couldn't get enough adrenaline into her bloodstream, I was actually convinced that I was going to die when I jumped out of that miniscule bi-plane, and spent the few weeks leading up to the big day utterly terrified and unable to sleep.

And the last time was Sunday, my birthday, which I spent with my bloke and my eldest daughter, both of whom are (I have come to realise) much braver than me. We went to Go Ape! which is a circuit high in some treetops in Buxton, Derbyshire, made up of rope ladders, cargo nets, bungee jumps, and zip wires, for visitors to make their way around while testing their strength of mind and character. I booked it because I wanted to have an exciting experience for my thirty-seventh birthday which didn't revolve around sitting in a pub with a load of people getting drunk, and I'm so glad that I did. Although when I booked, I had forgotten the fact that I suffer a little from vertigo.

An hour in, we reached a bridge of rope swings, hung between two trees about eighty feet in the air. My other half stepped across first, swinging wildly but pulling himself valiantly from one swing to the next until he reached the safety of the facing platform. My daughter went next, froze on the first plank of wood that wobbled violently in front of her, before harnessing her courage and managing to cross in just a few minutes. Then it was my turn – extreme sports extraordinaire. As I put my foot onto the first swinging log and grabbed onto the adjoining ropes that held it to the cable above, I made the mistake of looking beyond my feet and to the ground, way below me. My stomach went in to my mouth, my legs turned to jelly and I froze – completely.

Then I began to make strange wailing sounds that had never been emitted from my mouth before. It took me twenty minutes to cross just six feet of rope-bridge, with the aid of my very supportive and lovely family, who did not burst out laughing, but encouraged me every step of the way while I cried like a baby and tried not to throw up my breakfast.

There were many fun elements too, I must add, mainly the zip wires and 'Tarzan jumps' – all in all it was a brilliant day out. Facing the fear when you are terrified is a fantastic way to feel alive, and to remind yourself that pretty much anything is possible if you are prepared to meet that terror head-on and take it by the horns. There is nothing as satisfying as proving to yourself that, whatever life throws at you, you can tackle it by just putting your mind in to 'brave mode'.

You Only Get One Go at this Life – October 18th 2012

It's still dark outside. I have been up for nearly two hours, stirring to the sounds of the baby kicking against the wooden slats of her cot and gurgling to herself. I love lifting her from her bed first thing in the morning, seeing the flicker of recognition on her little pink face as she makes out my features in the green, half-light of her room, gently illuminated by the coloured nightlight in the corner.

She sat in her bouncy chair in the kitchen while I made her milk, smiling at me every time I looked her way and wriggling her tiny feet excitedly at the prospect of receiving her warmed bottle. Now she is back in her cot asleep, while Betty the dog is lying on her beanbag snuggled up close to the radiator, content because she has some company once again. I feel fully awake, the clock showing half past seven, the curtains still shut against the pitch black outside.

Since I gave up drinking, I never struggle to wake up in a morning (a good job as 6 a.m. is now considered a lie-in for the baby!). In the last two years, I have been ill once with a bad cold, but generally I feel fitter than I have ever felt in my life, with more energy than I know what to do with. I never crave a huge portion of carbs for breakfast either, which I regularly did when I drank alcohol. I remember quite frequently cooking up a greasy fry-up before work in order to soak up the hangover that I was pretending I didn't have.

That in itself seems bizarre now, when a bowl of cereal, some juice, and maybe a banana form the basis of my morning meal each day. The idea of gorging on a plate of greasy food laden with saturated fat turns my stomach! At work I would down endless cups of coffee and cans of Red Bull or Coke, just to try and stay alert, never considering that all those artificial means to prop myself awake would be totally unnecessary if only I stopped poisoning my body with alcohol each night.

I fell into such a blatant trap in my younger years but could never recognise it until I became teetotal; drinking to feel more confident, to have fun, to ward off the loneliness, to cope with stress, only to suffer the associated anxieties, depression, tiredness, mood swings, lack of confidence, and depleted energy levels. And then to rejuvenate my weary body and mind, what did I do? Pour more of the poison down my neck, feeling better for it initially (but only initially) because I was satisfying my cravings for a drug that I was addicted to.

The answer is so simple; remove the drug, remove the need for the drug. Just as in quitting smoking, where the desire for a toxic cigarette dissipates once the habit has been kicked, the cravings for alcohol just vanish as soon as you shift your perception about drinking it. I remember saying to someone years ago that I never wanted to become an alcoholic because then I would have to stop drinking for ever, which would be the most awful thing. Clearly I was already addicted to the stuff otherwise the notion of living without it wouldn't have worried me in the slightest. Time just cemented my addiction until I reached a point where alcohol would have killed me, one way or another, if I had continued to drink as I was during the last couple of years prior to quitting.

I wrote a lot when I first stopped drinking, just to help me organise my thoughts regarding alcohol and how I had reached such a low point in my life. I felt very sad to begin with at the thought that I was giving up my beloved wine. I recall writing one thing though which still sticks in my mind, which was that to die prematurely through drinking would, as well as being tragic for those left behind, be such a monumentally stupid reason for dying.

That seems even clearer to me now with eighteen months of sobriety behind me; to have lived life in a permanent stupor, hungover or drunk, depressed, anxious, and grumpy, only to die before time because alcohol had poisoned my body, would have just been the biggest waste of life. I wish that everybody who is living their life through the tainted lens of binge drinking could recognise what I, and others who have managed to become alcohol-free, can see so clearly; life is so precious and so short, that we should be able to remember and appreciate every day of it.

I know that if I had been drinking last night, I would have resented every minute that I spent with the baby so early this morning, cursing the fact that I had not been able to sleep the morning away. Instead, I cherished every second.

Rolling the Dice and Landing in New York City – October 21st 2012

When I was twenty-eight I flew to New York City with my daughter, then four years old, for a short break. I was newly divorced, had just finished my first degree in American History, and had absolutely no idea who I was or where my life was going. As the cab approached Manhattan from JFK Airport and I saw the skyline for the first time, grey and imposing against the freezing January sun, I cried. No place on earth has ever affected me in the way that New York did during those four days that I spent trudging around in sub-zero temperatures with my little girl on my shoulders, bundled up in a pink coat and white furry Russian hat.

We did the usual tourist stuff; Statue of Liberty, Empire State, Chrysler Building, and Greenwich Village, and we also visited the Bronx Zoo (I think we were the only ones silly enough to brave the cold that day, and virtually had the whole place to ourselves), after which we missed the bus back to Manhattan and had to sit for an hour by the roadside on the edge of the Bronx feeling more than a little apprehensive about our surroundings, if I'm brutally honest.

New York City felt like home to me as soon as I arrived. I had no qualms about getting up and out of the hotel on 5th Avenue as soon as the sun came up (major jetlag), bundled up in hats and big coats to ward off the cold, mingling amongst rushing commuters as they made their way to the office, and we made ours to a cosy diner we discovered that served great coffee and mammoth croissants. (I gave up asking for a four-year-old-girl-sized portion of anything after the first day – such a thing didn't exist and so we bought one of everything and shared).

The New Yorkers we met loved my little girl and fussed over her no end. We visited a shoe shop close by the Empire State Building and bought her some Timberland boots and thick socks in order to fight the winter cold a little more zealously than we had originally managed with a pair of totally inadequate wellington boots. The three men who staffed the shop were, upon first impression, a bunch of rude boys, collectively weighing in at around 1400 lbs. and dressed in football shirts and massive, baggy jeans.

They thought my daughter was the cutest thing they had ever seen, however, and tended to her every need with all the care and attention of her own grandma. The friendliness they displayed was reflected all over the city, in every shop and restaurant and public space we went. It was a magical few days, and just as I had cried when I arrived, I shed a few tears on the plane home as well, high above the Atlantic Ocean while my little girl slept peacefully next to me.

I am a different person now to the risk-taker I was back then. I wonder if, in some way, how I used to be was connected to my heavy drinking. The characteristics displayed by a person who is willing to risk her health and the security of her world by constantly getting drunk and exposing herself to dangerous situations, are perhaps the same characteristics that led me to flying to NYC on a whim with my little daughter, or to doing a skydive a couple of years later. During those years, I also packed in a secure job in order to start a business (thankfully it didn't flop), and then later sold that business to go back to university to do a law degree (again, the risk paid off and I got a 2:1 – thank God).

Prior to my daughter being born, I decided, again whimsically, to switch my university degree course (the first one) from Sheffield Hallam to East London University, to enable me to move in with my boyfriend of the time and his mates in Archway, North London. Then I fell in love, in a hurry, with my elder daughter's father and moved back up to Sheffield to be with him, had a baby, and got married.

Perhaps I didn't take the time to know myself sufficiently to find out what it was that would have made me happy in life. Pouring alcohol down my neck each time I was happy, or sad, or stressed, or celebrating – I never got in touch with the real me, and consequently every life-decision I made was based on something of a guess, like rolling a dice and just going with an arbitrary outcome, trusting my life to some passing fancy. In many ways I am grateful for the way that I was (not the boozy bit, but the associated decisions that I made in my life). For every negative I encountered as a result of drinking too much, I am lucky enough to have found myself in numerous situations that were amazing, fantastic life experiences – experiences that I would not have encountered if it weren't for the fact that I was a bit of a risk-taker. And, of course, being the way I was resulted in my wonderful first daughter being born.

Having said that, I wouldn't go back there today – I was lucky that the chances I took didn't backfire and bite me on the arse, and, ultimately, they were about short-term gratification and not ensuring a secure future for me or my daughter. I am a very different kettle of fish today; the way that I act and the decisions I take are based upon the consideration of what is best for all of us, me and my family (now doubled in size), and the implications – financial, emotional, and personal – are debated before committing to anything of any importance. In order to ensure any longevity of happiness, I believe that is the only way to live.

Of all the crazy stuff I got up to in my wayward, drink-fuelled days, however, visiting New York City remains one of my most treasured memories.

Goodbye Huge Pants – October 22nd 2012

Last week I wrote about switching the baby on to bottles, which she is now taking happily. This is a quick update for you.

I found some nice organic, extra-satisfying stuff for her bedtime feed which comes in a cute blue tin with pictures of the moon and stars on it. This (ridiculously) makes me feel happier about giving her formula instead of breast milk, because it's organic. I know, I know, I've done six months (almost) but such is the strength of the government's message about the superiority of breastfeeding that I still feel a bit guilty to be giving her the powdered variety, even this many months down the line. Anyway, it's done and she seems happy and well, so that's that.

As a result of finally reclaiming my body after almost a year and a half of baby-making and building, I had a rather lovely moment today – I chucked my massive, fat-strapped, thoroughly unsexy, non-underwired maternity bras in the bin; hurray!! Did anyone ever invent a viler undergarment than the maternity bra? I think not.

For the whole summer I struggled with what to wear. OK, I live in England and the weather is notoriously awful, but there were the odd few days here and there when I wanted to dress in something strappy and floaty (despite the fact that floaty isn't necessarily a good look when you are carrying that extra baby weight around your middle). Ignoring my bulging muffin top, I bought a couple of vest tops and one or two chiffon numbers, only to have any chance of them looking pretty ruined by the extraordinarily unfeminine, ultra-wide bra straps – ultra wide and a bit grey owing to being put through the wash too many times as a result of milk spillages and baby sick.

Thinking about it, someone did actually invent a viler undergarment than the maternity bra, because I threw a few of these away today too; the super-sized knicker. A few weeks after my caesarean, my new, wonky scar became slightly infected. 'No', the doctor informed me gently, 'it is not supposed to be that colour. Buy some massive pants, and make them really big – so that the elastic reaches your boobs.'

Off went the other half to Tesco and dutifully returned an hour later with a multipack of briefs (and I use that word in the loosest sense) that should never be worn by anyone under the age of eighty-five. I have never felt less attractive in my entire life than when I put those things on (a generous three sizes bigger than my usual and yet still a tad on the snug side) and teamed them with a grey, fat-strapped maternity bra, the enormous cup sizes almost matched by the bags under my poor, sleep-deprived eyes.

Today, all bras and massive pants took a flying nosedive in to the wheelie bin, and good riddance to the lot of them.

At the weekend I am going to purchase a sack full of nice, brand-new, delicate-strapped lingerie. Hallelujah.

Fright Night – October 28th 2012

I woke up this morning with a pounding headache. The baby cried in her cot for twenty minutes or so, a low-level grumble that gradually grew to a full throttle scream, forcing me to drag myself out of bed and bring her downstairs for her milk.

Last night, the other half and I went out in town for Halloween. It was rammed, the bars full to bursting with revellers in fancy-dress costumes, a malevolent exhibition of devils, witches, and ghosts, incongruously sipping pints of lager and smoking cigarettes in clusters in doorways and on pavements. After giving up the breastfeeding, I decided that a little glass of white wine would do no harm – after all, if I have managed to maintain my sobriety for almost two years, then surely I can't have had that much of a problem. I threw caution to the wind and got a large glass down my neck; I joined the masses, discarding my odd status as teetotaller.

As always happens when I and alcohol come together, one glass did nothing to satiate my thirst for that crisp, cold wine with the slight acidic tang, and so I bought another, and a third. I don't remember getting home, my memory blurs after an argument I had with the other half; he made the mistake of attempting to curtail my alcohol intake, and I let him know in no uncertain terms that this was something I should and would allow myself to do after all the sacrifices of having a baby and breastfeeding for months on end.

I was still dressed when I awoke at six this morning, which then became five owing to the autumnal hour reversing. My tongue felt as though it had doubled in size, furry and dry against the roof of my mouth. When I looked in the mirror my mascara had streaked across my cheeks, my over-sprayed hair was stuck up at all angles like a scarecrow's. I could smell alcohol on my own breath. The baby was an inconvenience, waking up so early and forcing me to cope with my debilitated physical state in such a hurried fashion. I wanted to sleep it off until noon. I crept out of bed, not wanting to wake her dad – I couldn't face the recriminations and tongue-lashing that I knew would be coming my way as a result of my behaviour last night.

I hated myself as I took each step carefully, ensuring I didn't trip in the darkness. I tried to smile and comfort the baby but she knew I was not myself and recoiled slightly when I lifted her from her bed.

My eyes stung, my head thumped, and my skin was slightly moist with the glistening sheen of clamminess. The extra strong coffee made my heart beat too fast and I had to fight hard to regulate my breathing. Serious dehydration is no laughing matter. After drinking the coffee too quickly, I felt a surge of bile rising in to my throat and threw up suddenly in to the kitchen sink, while the baby looked on, questioningly. I hated myself again. I started to cry, and she stared blankly as my tears rolled off my cheeks and on to the wooden floor.

You know this is fiction, I hope. My other half did go down town last night with his mates, and I stayed at home with his visiting sister, and both my lovely daughters. We watched *X Factor* and chatted. The baby woke up at 11 p.m., distressed, and we calmed her right down straightaway, coaxing her tears in to a smile within minutes. The dog became terrified and anxiety-stricken after a few fireworks exploded nearby; we settled and comforted her. We were all asleep by midnight, drifting away in to drug-free slumbers, recouping and recharging ready for another day.

I woke up at 5 a.m., opening my eyes and settling my gaze on the beautiful cherubic baby in the travel cot beside our bed (a bedroom reshuffle took place as the other half's sister is here for the weekend), watching her smile and stretch out her fat little hands to demonstrate her desire to be cuddled. I was instantly awake, feeling full of energy and happiness, ready to look after my family and to enjoy whatever the day might bring.

Later, when my other half described what the city centre was like last night, full of Halloween-inspired ghouls getting plastered, I remembered how I used to be all those months ago; that waking up each weekend and feeling as though I had some terrible illness, was utterly normal, a sacrifice that I was willing to make in order to drink alcohol. I would waste entire days, unable to achieve anything other than muddling through, coping, waiting for enough time to pass for the hangover to subside. I would snap at my eldest daughter, unwilling to spend time enjoying stuff together, unable to find the motivation to think of anything interesting to do.

I would worry about how much money I had spent the previous night, whom I had offended by saying something stupid, whom I had flirted with and made a fool out of myself in front of. I would fret about my health, worry that everyone would think I was an alcoholic and stupid, that I couldn't hold my booze like they could, that I was a lesser human being. And then I would go and buy a couple of bottles of wine and drink those to numb the misery.

Words cannot describe how happy I am that the first part of this blog post is fanciful imaginings, how grateful I am that I finally saw the light, and how wonderful it feels to know that I will never, ever spend another morning like the one described above.

Happy Memories of Electric Whisks – October 30th 2012

I was twenty-three and pregnant with my elder daughter when my grandma died. She had lived with my parents, my older sister, and me since I was nine years old, (together with my grandpa prior to his death, when I was sixteen). Even before my grandparents moved over to join us in Sheffield from their Lincolnshire bungalow, we were very close. My sister and I were thrilled when they, along with our parents, made the decision to buy a house in Sheffield and for us all to live together.

My grandma suffered from Alzheimer's disease in her last years, and when she finally passed away, she no longer knew who I was. I visited her in the nursing home where she saw out her final months when I was several months pregnant, and although she demonstrated happiness at the news of the impending baby, she had no idea that my soon-to-be-born daughter was her great-grandchild. She died soon after that visit.

Life moves on; my baby was born and I married my (now ex) husband a few months later. Although I was extremely sad that I had lost my beloved grandma, I was so caught up with the hectic schedule that accompanies being a new mum and wife that I buried my grief to a degree in order to concentrate on the here and now.

As the years went by, the memories became increasingly distant, pushed to the back of my mind. I began to drink heavily in my late twenties, attempting to anaesthetise myself against the pain of my divorce and the sadness I felt at being left to raise my daughter without her dad around. All the negative events that I had experienced during my life prior to then, including the death of my grandma, were gradually whittled away to become minor grievances, diluted by wine, numbed by my drunkenness.

Somewhere along the way, I stopped feeling.

When I gave up drinking alcohol, and the weeks of sobriety turned in to months, I began to think a lot about stuff that I had interred, long ago, in the depths of my consciousness. I became aware that most of the sad or painful life experiences which had occurred earlier on in my life had never been 'dealt with' – instead of feeling emotional pain, living it, working through it, and then moving forward, I had just drunk those emotions away, blotting them out like an eclipsed sun. I had, effectively, never known true pain.

I had lived through things as though I were an automaton, forbidding myself to feel emotions like a human being should, boxing painful memories away like disused ornaments in a dusty attic. Drinking took away my ability to hurt.

But slowly, emotions have returned. Over the last few months, particularly after the birth of my second daughter, I have thought of my grandma frequently (our baby is the namesake of my grandma and of my partner's mother). Silly things remind me of her; an M&S nightie hanging on an old lady's washing line; re-reading *Anne of Green Gables*; whipping cream to peaks with an electric whisk, mine being a modern version of the 1970s one I used to borrow from her as a child keen on baking; the new series of *Dallas*; attempting to sew my other half's trouser hems, minus the wonderfully equipped sewing box she kept so well stocked; Pond's face cream – the reason behind her lovely pink complexion; my baby's little chin, round like a button, and which so reminds me of her great-grandma's.

Although it has been fourteen years since her death, I still miss my grandma. I wish she could have known my two lovely girls, and seen my sister and I as mothers with our own families to look after. She gave us such constant and unconditional love, and I wish that I had been given the chance to visit her and look after her at an older age than that at which she passed away.

Although I still cry sometimes when I see the seemingly inane things that remind me of her, I am so glad that I feel those emotions and think of her so fondly, as often as I do. I wouldn't have ever grieved properly for her had I still been drinking wine every night, and, even though it hurts, I am happy to finally be dealing with my feelings, good and bad, like a fully functioning human being.

Letter to Me, 20 Years from Now – November 3rd 2012

I'm an atheist so I struggled with the concept of a higher power when I first gave up drinking. An alternative source of motivation to help me stay away from the booze came from an image I kept in my head of me in the future. A version of me that I would be proud to grow in to, rather than the grumpy, stressed piss-head I had turned into in the last few years that I spent drinking. I knew that I had to become that woman in my head, otherwise I would be letting myself down big time, and I couldn't stand living with that sense of failure. Below is a letter written to that imagined future me – the one who helped me get booze out of my life once and for all.

Twenty-two years ago you stopped drinking alcohol. Do you remember that chapter in your life, the drinking days? Does it stand out in your history as a definitive period, or has it now been consigned to the 'insignificant pile' of your memory?

Funny how, when you were in the middle of it all, you couldn't imagine another way, an alternative way of living. For years you thought you would always be a boozer, forever wasting your weekends in a haze of pinot grigio and chardonnay, constantly picking up the pieces after foolish nights out where you made an idiot of yourself again and again.

So, was ditching alcohol the right thing to do? Do you regard the making of that decision as a defining moment in your life? I suspect you do. If you hadn't made that choice, you more than likely wouldn't even be around to read this letter twenty years from now – and if you were, you'd be a physical wreck with your liver shot to bits, looking like shit to boot. I bet if you had continued to drink, you wouldn't be in a relationship either, certainly not with your beloved soul mate, the one you became engaged to in a tent in

Cornwall, June 2011. And if you hadn't embarked on the path of sobriety, you wouldn't have the wonderful joy of close relationships with your two girls, both of whom will be adults now and maybe with children of their own, making you a grandma.

Do you have that kind of relationship with them? Did you turn out to be the kind of mum that you always wanted to be?

When you stopped drinking it seemed like the only choice to make. Do you remember that moment of clarity when you woke up the morning after your last drunken episode, so full of self-hatred and remorse and fear, so fed up with failing to live up to your potential, and hell bent on climbing off that ride? Does it still haunt you – that feeling of being alone, terrified, and sliding down into oblivion without any certainty that you might discover a slip road, a route off the madness?

My guess is that life became a whole lot better, fuller, and happier in the times that followed 2011, the year you had your last drink. I imagine there will be a few regrets, but they won't be the sort that turn in your stomach like a rusty knife, gouging away at your inner soul and inflicting self-hatred over and over, like a relentless torturer. God, those mornings when you used to lie in bed, crying and cursing yourself, wishing that you could turn back the clock and wipe away the events of the previous night – do you still think of those times? I hope that, if you do, you think of them thankfully – that you regard them as the foundations of a new you, a better you, the right you. Because if those times hadn't happened, you never would have stopped drinking – it had to get that bad for you to put an end to it, once and for all.

In your mid-thirties, things were just coming together. You found optimism around that time, something that had been lacking previously. The future suddenly began to look attainable: bright and full of possibilities. I hope you managed to fulfil all the dreams that you formulated in that period when you first gave up alcohol.

Can you recall how much more energy and passion you discovered for everything post-booze, or has that just become a happy norm rendering you unable to remember ever being any different? It's funny to think that, in twenty years from now, the couple of decades you pissed up the wall boozing will be a distant memory to you. It probably won't even seem like you any more; the you that is together and fit and healthy, mostly happy and steady, dependable and predictable. I bet she won't recognise the old version – depressed, wallowing in negativity, drowning in wine and shame, and unable to find her place in the world. It's odd to imagine that the boozy you was something of a blip, you but with errors, a Lucy possessed by demons – demons that I hope you saw the back of.

Did you finally put all your ghosts to bed? Did you forgive yourself all those misdemeanours, the messed-up relationships and bad moods, the wrong turns you made here and there as you tried to navigate your way out of the labyrinth that alcohol abuse led you into?

My wish now, in November 2012, is that in twenty years you will look back over your life and see that boozed-up woman, the younger you in her teens through to mid-thirties, drinking, smoking, in denial, frightened, ashamed, loud-mouthed, terrified, nervous, anxiety-ridden, panic-stricken, an alcohol addict, and you will dismiss that chapter as a bit of a cock-up, a bump in an otherwise smooth road. My wish for you is that life without alcohol became the absolute norm.

At the time of writing, I think I am already profoundly different to who I was just two years ago, so who knows what the next twenty years will bring? I am no longer frightened to catch up with you, future Lucy. I trust you and when we eventually meet, I know you won't have let me down.

When Was the Last Time You Felt Really, Truly Lonely? – November 5th 2012

I lay alone in the dark, sensing that the bed was all mine. The clock said 8 p.m., but that made little sense to me – it had been morning not five minutes ago. Voices, barely audible, filtered in from the living room, and I remained still, my heart beating violently.

I was about thirty years old, stuck in between two relationships with two equally unsuitable men. One, an old friend, was someone I loved dearly but with whom I shared zero sexual chemistry; the other was his polar opposite – not very intellectual, a manual labourer, physically extremely attractive and a heavy drinker. Of course. Both were heavy drinkers.

For several months I had been pinballing to and fro between the two of them; the manual labourer doing nothing to stimulate me mentally, and so weekends spent with him would be followed by a desperate need to indulge in some food for the mind with the old friend, the one who was terribly intelligent and articulate, funny and kind, but for whom I felt nothing in a physical sense.

This particular weekend I remember feeling exceptionally confused and reckless, frustrated by the absence of a single man in my life who met all my needs, rather than these two semi-perfect partners.

On the Friday night I had gone to the pub with Mr Physical, played a bit of pool, drank large quantities of strong continental lager, and smoked too many fags. We'd returned to his flat late to discover his flatmate and a bunch of his friends pre-loading with shots in preparation for a party.

I remember walking in to the party later on with all those men, grabbing a beer and swaying a little while chatting to someone, anyone. That was about midnight, and then my memory goes black. So far, so familiar. On such occasions, I never intended to go out and get absolutely out of my skull on booze, it just kind of happened. One minute I felt OK, the next I would be waking up hours later as if I had been abducted and then unceremoniously dumped by a bunch of memory-zapping aliens. I could never remember a thing.

When I awoke at such an odd time, 8 p.m., in one of my unsuitable boyfriends' beds, I knew something really bad had happened, something that went beyond the norm. It didn't make sense that he wasn't there; it was extremely out of character for me to be waking at 8 p.m. – where the hell had the day gone?

I just lay in that big empty bed, staring at the ceiling, listening to his flatmate talking to someone in the living room. That feeling came again, the one that made me desperately want to crawl out of my skin and into someone else's, somebody good. I couldn't call anyone, I was too ashamed. How can you make it sound normal, that you have woken up a couple of hours before you should be going to bed, unable to remember anything? I had no idea what had happened, and I couldn't talk to anyone.

Whenever I wonder if I over-dramatised my alcohol dependency, whether I was just a social drinker who once in a while went a bit too far, I remember that night. I stayed on my own in his bed, wide awake, until the early hours of the following morning when he returned home, slightly drunk. My heart weighed a thousand tons, my eyes were dead with the resignation that I had done something that I wasn't sure I ever wanted to know about. The self-hatred gnawed at my insides like a rat. I never asked him what had happened; I couldn't bear to hear his answer.

That was the loneliest time of my entire life.

The Steam Mop – I Highly Recommend Buying One – November 8th 2012

I'm not sure if it was all that drinking I used to do, but recently it feels as though I raced through my twenties and early thirties as a young, immature, and somewhat irresponsible youth before waking up on the other side of thirty-five as a proper grown-up. Something in particular brought this home to me earlier on this week: my purchase of an electric steam mop.

My other half, lovely as he is, is not the most domesticated chap I have ever met. By way of an example, when I ask him to clean the kitchen sides after cooking dinner, he tears off a scrap of kitchen roll and slides it back and forth across the surfaces a couple of times, minus any detergent, soapy water, or anything else that may constitute a hygienic, germ-killing aid.

So you may appreciate that he was not quite as excited as I was when a man delivered a large cardboard parcel a couple of days ago, which contained my new Groupon bargain buy: the steam mop. I, on the other hand, couldn't wait to tear open the box, fill that sucker up with water, plug it in, and get steam-mopping! Earlier that day, I even (this is how sad I am, and how obsessed with cleaning) deliberately, and somewhat joyfully, left the dog's muddy footprints and a few pram-wheel streaks on the floorboards, purely for the purpose of getting the maximum effect from my clever new device.

I was very pleased to see the steam emitting from the mop head after just thirty seconds, as promised on the instructions, and even more so when I witnessed the ease with which my new cleaning device cut through that dirt, as if assisted by the most powerful of bleaches (which it wasn't, it just does it with steam – amazing!) Back and forth I went, the dog and baby looking on in amazement. I could almost hear what they were thinking: "How gleaming that wooden floor looks! How fast and efficient that machine is! It's truly wondrous."

Afterwards, as I reclined in the chair with a cup of herbal tea, admiring my handiwork and that lovely new gadget leaning up against the wall, its work (for today) now done, it did occur to me that I am indeed a true grown-up. I get my kicks out of steam-mopping my kitchen floor. I am excited by hygiene, fulfilled by the purchasing of a bargain cleaning product.

There was a time when all my spare cash went on bottles of wine, and I only felt excitement if unlimited booze and a full packet of twenty fags formed the basis of my evening's entertainment. Not so these days – now that I'm a responsible adult, it's all about spending my disposable income on an electric steam mop (you should buy one if you haven't already; they are a truly wonderful invention), and finding thrills in the shininess of my wooden kitchen floor.[4]

My Thoughts on Being Teetotal Before I Saw the Light – November 10th 2012

I wrote this about a year and a half ago, when I first gave up alcohol. I knew that I couldn't drink any more because of the destructive and dangerous effect it was having on me, but I wasn't happy about it. Reading this, I remember just how much I was dreading spending the rest of my life without booze.

I'm so happy that the feelings I write about here didn't last all that long. There is a lot of writing here, and a lot of it I still stand by – how society in general has a lot to

---

[4] If you do buy one, be careful that you don't slip over on your exceptionally polished floor if wearing just socks. I went flying yesterday after a mammoth steam-mopping session and bruised my coccyx.

answer for in terms of making it very hard to even contemplate becoming teetotal, for instance. But the negativity I felt back then about ditching alcohol is long gone; these days I couldn't be happier that I don't (and will never again) touch booze.

May 2011

A counsellor, whom I visited for a while in the months that followed my acrimonious and emotionally devastating divorce, once said to me that he thought there was no truth in my belief that ordinary life (that being daily, routine tasks that we all undertake such as going to work, supermarket shopping, and cleaning the bathroom) was a bit dull. The point that I was trying to make was that my excessive drinking and (by then, long abandoned) hedonistic days of raving had (or still did in the case of alcohol consumption) provided a longed for, and indeed psychiatrically beneficial, respite from the daily grind, and that life sans such escapist indulgences seemed, well, a bit dull. The point that my therapist was attempting to convey was that if a person's life is sufficiently fulfilled, the need to derive pleasures from artificial means such as drugs and booze is simply eradicated.

A nice thought and one which, eight years on, I am still striving to prove true in my search for self-fulfilment and happiness. But a thought nonetheless which stirs a niggling doubt in the back of my sober mind – that once a person has exposed herself to such highs and freedom from self-consciousness and inhibitions, it becomes very difficult to ever go back.

Human beings have always sought relaxation from the stresses of life, the source of that relaxation stemming from a wide variety of legal, illegal, morally acceptable, and socially frowned upon substances as remedies for a little escapism. The need, then, to flee from everyday life is not a new phenomenon, despite the moral panic that has escalated in recent years regarding alcohol abuse and 'booze Britain'.

During the Gin Crisis of the eighteenth century (as depicted in Hogarth's painting of the same name) it was thought that, on average, Londoners were imbibing roughly a pint of gin every week, an amount that sounds shocking to me – and I have drunk a fair old amount of alcohol in my time. Drugs, too, are not a twentieth-century invention and it is believed that mind-altering substances have been taken since the days of the Stone Age. Drug paraphernalia was discovered a few years ago on the Caribbean island of Carriacou, which dates back to somewhere between 100 and 400 BC. Drugs consumed such a long time ago were probably not taken for the recreational purposes that people take them today – rather they were more likely to have been used to actuate spiritual, trance-like states of mind. But still, the need to temporarily adjourn from the norm has been with humankind for thousands of years.

In the twenty-first century we are subject to contradictory social values, not least in the arena of drug and alcohol abuse. The hypocritical nature of the media and government when dealing with the issue of alcohol (in particular) is noticeable all around us. I became teetotal in April 2011 and living without booze has brought the double standards and contradictions home in a stark way. Chavs are bemoaned for their frequent imbibing of alcopops, while middle-class dinner party goers are forgiven for their excessive consumption of merlot, barolo, and bordeaux. Politicians are quick to berate the youth of England for their delinquent, alcohol-driven behaviour witnessed each weekend on the nation's city streets, and yet the government's Responsibility Deal, introduced in the summer of 2010, in an effort to tackle the country's growing drinking problem, appears to have been reduced to little more than a series of half-baked undertakings.

Supermarkets have been instructed to label 80% of bottles and cans containing alcohol with details of their alcoholic content by 2013, and the advertisement of alcoholic products within 100 metres of schools has been banned. But issues such as inappropriate marketing, curbing licensing hours, and introducing a price per unit method costing structure[5] were thrown off the agenda and never even discussed.

The fact that several key members of the drinks industry make up the group is notable, and even more notable is the fact that the Royal College of Physicians, Alcohol Concern, the Institute of Alcohol Studies, the British Medical Association, the British Liver Trust, and the British Association for the Study of the Liver all expressed an inability to support the Responsibility Deal due to their belief that the compromised agenda of the group would do nothing to help stem the growing tide of alcohol-related illnesses and premature deaths in the UK.

Alcohol is ubiquitous. With ad buffers on the TV (*Come Dine With Me*), in-your-face promotional offers for cheap beer and wine in supermarket aisles, TV programmes, and films that feature alcohol being knocked back like water, and which often normalise and celebrate getting drunk, it is almost impossible not to think that everyone is out there getting pissed on a regular basis, and that it is completely OK.

Drinking is so revered in our culture that I, as a non-drinker, have become an oddity for not partaking in it. I have been expelled from a club, a club that I took

---

[5] These were thought by many in the health sector to have the potential to impose a real impact on alleviating the alcohol problem, and highlighted in a report by the University of Sheffield which was published in *The Lancet* medical journal. (*The Lancet*, Volume 375, Issue 9723, 17–23 April 2010, Pages 1355–1364.)

completely for granted when I drank alcohol. If you are square, the school swot all grown up, a quiet sort who does not feel the need to show off at parties, you were never invited to join.

But if a hedonistic streak rules your social persuasions and you are usually found amongst the loud, cigarette-smoking, steadily-becoming-drunker-and-drunker brigade in the back garden of the house party, then yes, you are most definitely in the club. Of course, temporary exclusion is an option; pregnancy, a course of antibiotics, major illness – these are all *bona fide* reasons for fleetingly bowing out of the club. Giving up alcohol because you are not in control of it, because it has affected an unshakeable grip on you, because you never want to allow a single drop of it near your lips ever again for fear of it killing you – these are reasons that are tantamount to a lifelong exclusion.

Can I say, hand on heart that I am happy to be relegated to membership of the squares' club, hangin' with the fuddy duddies? Stuck in the corner with the grey-haired and the ankle biters, sipping a mineral water while sneaking frequent peeks at my watch to find out how long I must wait before I can politely leave? No, I can't. It still doesn't feel like me, to be cast out from the mouthy drunks who dance wildly and laugh too loudly at the Best Man's rubbish speech, and who huddle outside smoking and discussing some gossip that seems far more significant than it ever does the next day.

I spent all of my adult life (and most of the transitional years between childhood and full maturity too) as a fully paid-up member of that group, amounting to two-thirds of my life. Leaving that significant element of my being behind is taking some major re-acclimatisation.

For the most part, I have taken the easy way out since I made the choice to become teetotal, hence my growing fancy for *Come Dine with Me* and other variations of meaningless televisual distraction – staying at home sober is definitely preferable to going out and staying sober, although I hope it won't always be that way. I have found it much harder to say goodbye to the old me than I ever imagined, and equally difficult to become acquainted with the personality left behind in her absence.

When engaged in activities that never involved drinking copious amounts of booze (i.e. spending time with my daughter in the park, meeting friends for coffee, going to the cinema – although I have to admit that the last one was usually sandwiched between a couple of pre-film beverages and a skinful afterwards), the issue of losing my membership of the formerly beloved drinkers' club does not rear its ugly head. That's my safety zone.

I heard a lyric on the radio the other day that has stuck in my mind; Bruce Springsteen's 'Better Days', in which he sings 'But it's a sad man my friend who's livin' in his own skin, and can't stand the company.' What came first – hating my own company and drinking to obliterate it, or drinking until I hated the person it turned me into? The booze that is sold to us through advertising and the media is not a substance I recognise; happy images of laughing friends sharing a bottle of wine over nibbles.

Alcohol has disappointed me and left me with something of a sense of being cheated, mis-sold. It has taken many years to realise it, but alcohol is not for me and it does nothing for me other than turn me against myself. It robs me of my self, and, in becoming sober, I have discovered that my self, well, it's not that bad after all. It has taken a few weeks but I am beginning to see that the years I spent drinking was time spent trying to run away from myself. I hated myself and of course the vicious circle of drinking, self-loathing, drinking, self-loathing, only serves to exacerbate this.

When I first embarked upon this new, sober chapter in my life, I took it for granted that the key to all my problems in life lay with alcohol – after years of abusing the stuff, it made sense to herd all the negativity I had experienced in to one box, label it 'Booze' and close the lid on it. I began to do some research on the subject, mainly by searching the internet for alcohol dependency, how to give up drinking, female alcoholism and recovery from addiction. My search criteria screamed out 'Help!' to anyone who could guide me out of the mire that I had spent so long floundering in.

In addition to the various websites and books I scoured, I talked honestly and frankly to friends who I knew had their own addiction issues, and gradually I began to piece together a picture of the alcohol-influenced world that we all inhabit. After giving up drinking in April 2011, it soon became apparent to me that I needed to gain a fuller understanding of alcohol, why it has been so attractive to me, why it retains such a hold on me, as though it were a particularly desirable but destructive lover who I just cannot leave behind.

I cannot bear the thought of spending the remainder of my time on earth with booze lurking around my thoughts, a tormenting presence that is constantly propositioning me. I loathe the idea that I might always be yearning and desperately craving its magic, and yet must never allow myself to give into temptation for fear of the consequences.

And so I decided to start writing – to construct a convincing and lasting argument for myself and anyone else out there who has seen their souls ravaged by the demon drink, pertaining to why a life without alcohol can be fulfilling and happy and not at all boring, and why, in the end, going teetotal is the best choice to make for those who are unfortunate enough to be saddled with the misguided belief that one drink is never enough.

To Regret Deeply Is to Live Afresh – November 11th 2012

I write for many reasons, often because I find it easier than talking to people. Sometimes because it is the only method I know of bringing emotions out of myself in a way that helps me cope with them more helpfully and productively.

Last night as I sat talking to my teenage daughter, who is now as tall as me (a fact which she takes great delight in pointing out to her mum on a regular basis), I found myself looking beyond her thirteen-year-old form back to her childhood. Her words kept tumbling out, but in my head I was seeing and listening to her at four, five – small and innocent and totally trusting.

I recalled us sitting together on the high bed in her attic bedroom in an old house of ours, the walls bubblegum-pink and furry toys scattered around the floor. It was bedtime and we were reading a story as we did every night. Except that night I was overwhelmed with depression; a foul, black mood swamped me like a heavy cloak, rendering me incapable of breaking free from its negativity.

I had struggled all day with a debilitating hangover and desperately wanted to crack open the wine that sat downstairs in my fridge. I barked the words of the book at my little girl, racing through the story-telling at breakneck speed; no silly voices, no humorous play-acting, no deliberate creation of suspense through dramatic pauses, or varying intonation. Just the sound of my monotone, depressed voice, almost shouting the words out to her while she sat by my side, listening gratefully.

Of course, when she was little, my daughter never saw me really drunk; I wasn't lying on the settee day and night clutching a bottle of vodka in my hand. I got up at 7 a.m. each day, hangover or not, got her ready for school, fed the cat/gerbils/rabbit (whichever we had at the time), took her to school, went to work, muddled through, picked her up from school, walked home, cooked dinner, put her to bed. I did all those things. I functioned.

But there were many times when I didn't give her what she desperately needed as a little girl; my unadulterated attention – me without the tormenting presence of addiction niggling in the darker reaches of my consciousness; me who read her a story in an entertaining and fun way, present and attentive and not possessed by the thought of that bottle of wine in the kitchen.

But you can't unpick the past and re-stitch it in a better way.

Last night, as she talked to me about her day at school, I was so overcome with sorrow at what I had thrown away all those years ago, that I had to excuse myself, fleeing upstairs to the bedroom where I cried for just five minutes – stifled, secretive, agonising tears, shed because I will never be able to go back to my little girl that night, and read her the story in the way that she deserved. It is, quite simply, one of my biggest regrets.

On that note, and because I try to turn every negative in to a positive, I would like to share this quote with you, on the matter of regret:

"Make the most of your regrets; never smother your sorrow, but tend and cherish it till it comes to have a separate and integral interest. To regret deeply is to live afresh."

Henry David Thoreau

Sunday Mornings Are Great When You Don't Drink – November 12th 2012

Reasons why it's great not drinking

1. I got up at 6.30 a.m. (baby duties) and felt great, even after just 7 hours sleep.

2. I gave baby her bottle and then went for a 10k run with the dog. There was nobody around except us, and we covered three parks, all bathed in beautiful early morning sun.

3. I have no regrets from last night, no arguments to undo, no bad behaviour to apologise for.

4. No hangover.

5. I don't crave a massive plateful of greasy carbs for breakfast, thus screwing up my healthy eating plan.

6. I am not worried about all the money I spent last night, because I didn't spend a single penny.

7. My family is happy and well looked after.

8. Even after getting up so early, I look better and younger than I have in years.

9. I am happy.

10. I like myself.

Vice No More – November 14th 2012

I have come to realise that I have an addictive personality.

It was pointed out to me last night by my other (read, better) half, that I stare at my phone way too much. Upon hearing this, I had a bit of a strop, flounced off upstairs to take a bath (as an aside, with a great bath bomb thing shaped like a little Christmas pudding) and, after sulking for ten minutes, came to the realisation that my beloved actually had a point.

I didn't like to admit this to myself. (It has been said that I take criticism badly.) It still rankles when I remember my parents telling me to apologise to someone after a fall-out when I was little ... ow, the pain and humiliation of saying sorry!! I am a lot better these days, however, and I scuttled downstairs (after leaving my darling phone in the bedroom) to make amends.

I have to say, once the deed had been done and the iPhone dispatched to my bedside table, I experienced a freeing sensation. I didn't feel the need to constantly flick my eyes to the side to take a quick peek at the screen. I concentrated fully on the conversation I had with my elder daughter (she is also a phone addict and is currently facing a proposed household post-dinner phone amnesty with fear and trepidation), we caught up with American *X Factor*, and discussed it with zest and enthusiasm (we don't get out much), rather than interspersing our viewing with frantic button pushing and finger scrolling. It was a relaxing time.

So, yet again, I must admit that my other half was right.

It's getting to be pretty vice-free, my life these days. The booze has gone, as have the fags, no phone after dinner (until bedtime of course − got to catch up with my tweets at some point!!), very little chocolate, and Jason Vale's vegetable juices for breakfast.

I hardly recognise myself. I know what it is to feel contentment.

How Addiction Works – November 18th 2012

Big changes stem from small decisions, which in turn derive from a multitude of thought processes, some monumental and others seemingly insignificant. I see the world differently today from the way I did a couple of years ago; my eyes take in an alternative universe, a place which is poles apart from the world I once thought I lived in.

Being addicted to something that ruins you is a pretty difficult way to live. When I was a teenager I was hooked on starving myself, obsessed by skipping meals and weighing myself, throwing up on purpose, and counting the days that had passed since I last ate.

I once got dragged along to the doctor's by a well-meaning friend who thought I really should get help, but I suffered a panic attack in the waiting room which in turn brought on a gushing nose bleed, and so I ran outside to the car and never went back.

I resolved that issue when I found myself pregnant with my elder daughter. It suddenly dawned on me that the human body is quite remarkable and I loved mine for being able to nourish and grow this tiny life inside it. The urge to starve myself disappeared.

New motherhood meant that cigarettes and alcohol fell by the wayside too, until the onslaught of my divorce a few years later hit me like a train, tugging at the destructive seeds of self-harm that had been lying dormant all those years, poking and teasing them out until they emerged slowly, but full of vigour, from where they'd been hiding.

Then came the booze addiction, which was far more tenacious than the eating disorder. It became entrenched in my conscience and mindset, it defined who I thought I was, becoming the reason why I did anything and everything, the motivation for the choices I made. It was the driving force behind my selection of friends and boyfriends and the path I followed in life.

I didn't know I was addicted to alcohol, and so its insidious and altogether socially acceptable qualities enabled it to creep up on me unawares, pulling me down a dark and dangerous road, all the while soothing and comforting me and making all the pain seem normal. A persistent voice in my head told me that I was not a good person and that all the bad stuff that happened was down to some inherent characteristic of mine. The doomed relationships, financial struggles, unsatisfying jobs, failure to make something out of myself – I reasoned them all away by telling myself that I was not worthy of the good stuff.

It's easy to keep on hurting yourself if you believe you are no good. And, I have to be honest, there is something oddly comforting in being a misery in that way – you know where you are, right at the bottom, and so you figure you can't go any lower. You fight the fight each day with a willing acceptance that things can't get any worse, and anyway, there's always the alcohol to numb feelings when things really hit the fan. You can derive comfort from knowing that you don't belong in that cosy, false reality that is so ubiquitously present in Hollywood films and top up your diminishing pride by relishing being The Outsider. It bolsters the belief that you deserve to get drunk, because nobody understands you anyway and nobody truly cares.

You're trapped in one of those steel-jaw contraptions used by hunters; when the jaws slam shut around your leg any struggle to escape results in ripped tendons and unintentional amputations – a one-man bloodbath created by the trapped animal fighting to the end to get free and ultimately shredding itself to ragged streamers of flesh.

It takes years to find one's self ensnared in that way, and then all of a sudden there you are – stuck in that awful place, knowing neither how you arrived nor how to escape.

Big changes stem from small decisions, which in turn derive from a multitude of thought processes, some monumental and others seemingly insignificant.

Little thoughts begin to niggle at the back of your mind, a notion here, and an idea there. Over time you begin to act on them and the way that life changes around you as a result, how you find yourself featuring in different scenarios and discovering that you actually enjoy them, these things make a dent in the way you act; they begin to shape your new design.

And just as it takes an eternity for life to unravel in such a way that you finish off caught in the jaws of a steel trap, so it takes time to wind itself in and unfurl all over again in a completely new and ameliorated form.

Reactions need to occur, and behaviours be given the chance to draw a response from people around you. It's self-esteem that's required; that's the key to breaking out of the addiction cycle and starting afresh.

Self-esteem, self-respect, and self-confidence; the three amigos that shape the souls of happy people.

Bad Clothes Bought When Hungover, Off to a New Home – November 20th 2012

You definitely think more clearly when you don't get drunk every night. I know that sounds like the most glaringly obvious statement that I have ever typed, but sometimes I notice how differently I go about the business of living now that I'm not cracking open the pinot at wine o'clock each night.

I've sorted out my clothes over the course of the last week, flogging a load on eBay and chucking the rest to a charity shop. Clothes that made me wince every time I opened my wardrobe door, and clothes that I weighed up with one eyebrow cocked, pondering when, if ever, I might dare to wear them again, and clothes that resembled the sails on windsurfs, worn during weightier times.

These were garments that I mostly bought in moments of frantic indecision after roaming the city centre for hours on end, growing increasingly desperate and finally grabbing something that I would never normally wear in a month of Sundays, telling myself during those last moments of hasty 'retail therapy' that the outfit/top/jeans looked great. Until I got it/them on in front of my own mirror, that is, and the truth could no longer shield itself from me – I looked hideous.

In times gone by (the dark days of drunkenness) I didn't have the energy for attending to such matters; clothes got stacked up in my wardrobe like a Boxing Day sales rack in a department store. Stuff that I simply never wore, shoes left in their boxes, tags hanging off labels, outfits never put together.

I used to buy an awful load of crap too when I was hungover. Patience wasn't a noticeable virtue of mine when faced with the task of shopping for new threads amongst the heaving masses, all the while nursing a throbbing head and an unnatural craving to consume yet more greasy food and frothy, extra-shot lattes. Town on a Saturday afternoon is not the place to be when one is suffering from low blood sugar levels, forced to dawdle along behind hordes of casual browsers when the only thought on your mind is locating food with an excessive degree of carbohydrate content as quickly as possible in order to ram it down your throat.

Given that I no longer shop in this way (I am attempting, in my thirty-eighth year, to master the art of 'capsule wardrobe shopping' thus making just a few well thought-out investment buys that can be mixed and matched in a cohesive and stylish fashion), I decided to overhaul my bulging stock of unworn clothes in order to make room for a few garments that I might actually enjoy wearing.

And so yesterday I found myself experiencing a sense of accomplishment and satisfaction in the post office as I bundled off a few of my old 'rushed' purchases to a buyer somewhere in the West Midlands, resulting in a bit of extra money in my bank account and about half a foot more space in my wardrobe. The cash is being spent on my elder daughter's bedroom makeover, that in itself giving me a positive feeling of doing the right thing and making one of my beautiful girls very happy. (The other one is happy too, but her needs are met a little more simply at the moment; milk, clean nappy, cuddles, sleep.)

Oh, the joy of knowing that you are back in the driving seat of your life!

Happiness – November 23rd 2012

Does it sound evangelical to say that I felt complete joy and happiness last night as I pushed the baby's pram up a steep hill in the driving rain, no hood or hat protecting my head from the precipitation and howling gales, and the baby unable to see me or anything else owing to her rain cover being totally misted up with condensation? If I'm honest, I did feel a momentary pang of 'urrghh this is utterly horrible and miserable and I want to be at home in dry clothes, under a blanket in front of the TV'. But only for a minute, and then I reminded myself that I am living and this is what life is about sometimes; taking the dog for a walk in cold, wet weather in the dark.

Everyone tells you that alcohol is a depressant, and you know it's true, but somehow it's easy to push that to one side and imagine that your lack of real happiness stems from life just being a bit rubbish.

When you stop drinking alcohol for good, you can experience something akin to an evangelical awakening – moments of happiness that border on delirium, as you realise that you are alive, and lucky for all that you have, and that you've survived stuff and emerged out the other side strong and full of vigour.

I feel joy at seeing the sunrise, listening to the baby wake up, gurgling and burbling to herself in her cot, hearing a song that I love, going for a good run and knowing that I am growing in strength and stamina, having a coffee and a chat with a friend, cooking a new recipe, and eating the results.

I am happy nearly every day, at least for most of every day. I do get a bit grumpy or tired, occasionally a little stressed if I'm having a particularly busy and fraught day, but that's just the normal human experience – I would be a robot if I never felt those things. Generally though, I am on an even keel and happiness is the mainstay of my emotions.

I know that's because I don't drink alcohol. It's as simple as that. Drinking turned me against myself and created an internal battle of depression, anxiety and self-pity versus normality. Giving it up has allowed the real me to emerge, and the real me is happy and optimistic, calm and centred, full of creativity and determination and passion.

I am eternally grateful that I gave myself the chance to discover who I really am.

My Big Idea – November 25th 2012

A couple of months after drinking my final glass of booze I was sitting on the settee in my boyfriend's house attempting to summon up the courage to tell him about my BIG IDEA. I'd recently decided to start writing a blog (which ultimately became this one) but had also been mulling over the concept of a social network site for 'women like me' – i.e. those who wished they could put an end to the misery of an alcohol dependence but who had no idea where to start. Half of me felt that this notion was completely brilliant, and the other feared that my boyfriend (and untold numbers of strangers) would consider me stark raving bonkers for dreaming up such a thing.

For my whole life, or certainly my adult life, I thought small. I somehow never mustered the self-belief to really aim high, so when I was eighteen and thought I might like to work with children I didn't think about becoming a teacher but a nursery nurse instead (in the end I did neither). When I first dipped a toe into the world of employment, post-divorce, it was a temping agency and a series of low-paid administration jobs that I took on. And when I had the initial glimmer of an idea for creating an online source of help for binge-drinkers who wanted to sober up, I only took it as far as writing a blog – initially.

Then I thought about how big it could be and how many more people could be reached if my project became a worldwide social network instead. What could be achieved if I aimed high for once, really high.

That's when I became fixated on the notion of Soberistas.com, and, much to my surprise, my boyfriend did not burst out laughing when I described my plans to him as we sat together in his old house. Conversely, he told me I should go ahead and that he would help as much as possible.

So we did it.

Tomorrow, Soberistas.com will launch. It's nerve-wracking but at the same time I absolutely know there is a need for this website. One of the worst aspects of being a dependent and out-of-control drinker for me was that I felt so alone. It seemed that everyone I knew could drink without landing themselves in terrible trouble as I always seemed to do. None of my friends had ever been bundled into a cab, unconscious and fighting the urge to throw up everywhere. Nobody whom I socialised with drank so much that they mortally embarrassed both themselves and everyone around them, and then woke up the following day filled with self-hatred and a desire to run for ever from their reality.

But logically I know that it's not just me who acts this way in response to alcohol, and so one of the functions of Soberistas.com, I hope, will be to help people realise they are not alone. And in understanding that fact, a person feels instantly less desperate.

In building a community of like-minded people, I believe that one of the biggest battles in beating the booze can be fought. Solidarity; understanding that you aren't crazy just for being the way you are; being able to get support around the clock from the bedroom or lounge, or on your phone or laptop – all of that will, I'm convinced, help reinstate self-esteem and self-belief and simultaneously eliminate feelings of shame and guilt. Subsequently, it will become easier to find the strength to stop drinking, or at least I think, and hope, that will be the case. It's a safety in numbers issue.

Tomorrow is the very first day of Soberistas.com – I truly hope it helps.

Opportunities – December 1st 2012

Giving up alcohol has had many positive effects on my life. It takes time and patience to discover what hidden gems are hiding behind the pretence that alcohol cloaks your being with, but as time goes by I notice things that are truly exciting, as though life is starting again but this time it's being played out in a happy place.

One of the most striking differences between now and then is how the world has begun to open up, like a flower unfurling beneath a blazing sun. If you drink on a regular basis, and you drink until you are inebriated, your world closes down. Opportunities are shut off to you because you are incapable of thinking further than when that next drink is coming.

My days, my life, centred around wine; everything was a precursor to booze, so a walk in the countryside was nice but only because it led up to a cosy pint in a pub; a romantic meal in a restaurant I always enjoyed, particularly because it involved at least a couple of bottles of expensive red, followed by a liqueur, and then a few drinks in a late bar. Christmas, fantastic to spend time with the family, but you know what Christmas is great for – getting hammered and nobody really noticing, the one time of year when it's fully acceptable to go out and drink to your heart's content (or stay in and do the same).

But when the drink dries up, your horizons expand. Days cease to be about counting the hours until the wine can be uncorked, and become instead yet more hours in which new experiences can be tried, plans can be hatched, and projects can be developed. Sheffield all of a sudden seems small. It's really a great city, but in recent months I have become aware of how familiar it is to me; there aren't many corners of it that I don't know and I have begun to fantasise about living elsewhere, travelling, experiencing new cultures, spreading my wings. I want to grow.

Great achievements have been accomplished by human beings down the generations because of how we operate when we aren't sozzled. People have always drunk, but momentous inventions, life-changing leadership, and innovative architecture and design were not dreamt up by those who were perpetually sloshed.

I am filled with a passion and a drive for living that has grown slowly over the last couple of years, ever since I stopped drinking alcohol. It pushes me to do things that I would have previously shied away from, propels me to want more from the world.

When people talk about giving up drinking, they often focus on the immediate benefits: improved health, and the chance of living longer and healthier lives, better state of mind, more money, more balanced home life – when I knew that I wanted to quit drinking for good, these were the things that I was striving for and hoping would occur as a result of becoming teetotal. But the way in which the world opens up and becomes a cornucopia of never-ending possibilities, that to me is the greatest gift I have found in ending my destructive relationship with alcohol.

How to Do a 10k Race (and How not to) – December 2nd 2012

Today I ran my first 10k race in ten years. The race, known as the Percy Pud, takes place in the Loxley Valley, Sheffield, bypassing the beautiful Damflask reservoir. 1000 runners enter, with many turning up in Christmas-themed outfits, and each runner receives a Christmas pudding upon completion.

I last ran the Percy Pud when I was twenty-seven years old or thereabouts. I was in the throes of divorcing my elder daughter's dad, caught in the turbulent winds of an incredibly acrimonious split. My alcohol consumption had begun to creep up around that time, and I was regularly drinking enough to feel tipsy most nights, enough to get completely out of it two or three nights a week.

Somehow (maybe because I had youth on my side) I managed to turn up on time to run the Percy Pud and actually achieved a new personal best. The night before I had drunk four pints of Guinness and went to bed about 2 a.m. I ran the race in forty-eight minutes, fighting the desire to throw up all the way around.

To celebrate, a few of us went to a pub and got drunk.

Today was a different affair. Last night I put thought into what I ate (carbs – macaroni cheese), drank loads of water, and got an early night. I did a little run yesterday, just to work my muscles gently, but otherwise I rested (as much as you can with a seven-month-old and a teenager who requires an on-tap taxi service) in an effort to conserve my energy.

I ran the Percy Pud today in fifty-five minutes, a time which I am pretty pleased with. I didn't run for several months while pregnant and then subsequently recovering from the caesarean, and began to jog regularly about four months ago. I'm justifying my race time to you here, because a tiny bit of me really wanted to prove that by living a much healthier lifestyle, I would be able to easily smash my Personal Best.

But, the important thing is this – all the way round the race today, I was soaking up the beautiful scenery, enjoying the camaraderie of all the other runners, focusing my mind on breathing, my technique, running through the pain barrier. I ran it and I was there, in the moment – I lived that race. The last time I ran it, I was trying not to be sick and pushing myself to get to the finishing line so that I could get my Christmas pudding and get the hell out of there and off to the pub.

Thus, I am proud of what I did today, and have decided to buy a training book to help me improve my time and technique in 10ks. There's another race at the end of February 2013, and I'm aiming to get my PB down to less than forty-five minutes for that one.

Tonight I feel physically tired, the kind of tired you get when you have really pushed yourself, conquering the inner you that wants to slow down and instead forcing your legs to keep moving as fast as you can make them go. The calmness and ability to relax that physical exertion brings, is noticed and appreciated far more when sober.

Finding Me – December 9th 2012

How do we ever know who we are supposed to be? Which

version of us is the real one, and which are fabrications of our imaginations, finely tuned by our habits and daily living?

An advert for the Christmas film *Elf* played on the TV earlier. The voiceover set out the premise of the story as being about an elf who finds out one day that he isn't the person he grew up thinking he was. Armed with this truth, he decides to travel to New York to meet his dad and discover exactly who he is.

And hearing these words, I began to think that this kind of narrative is popular with people because it is a phenomenon to which many of us can relate. Maturity has much to do with self-discovery and exploration of self, but I think for those of us who have lived through and emerged out the other side of addictions, the need and desire to understand ourselves is particularly strong.

As a regular and heavy drinker, I thought I was outgoing, flirtatious, bubbly, a little bit of a daredevil, something of a maverick. As a sober person, my opinion of myself has altered drastically. I found out that I am not much of a party animal in actuality – the excessive socialising served as a cloak by which to disguise my urge to go out and get hammered. It was an easier pill to swallow if I got drunk with other people who were also getting sloshed, rather than staying home alone with just a couple of bottles of wine for company.

I'm much more interested in politics and humanity at large than I ever thought I was back in my drinking days. I simply had no energy to care about the world outside of my small and mostly inebriated existence. I now love setting myself challenges and achieving my goals, especially in running and creative projects; it is so rewarding seeing things come to fruition after hard work and planning. Pre-sobriety, running was a bit of a chore, something I did to keep in shape. I enjoyed it when I actually managed to go, but I didn't have the same passion for it as I have now. And creativity wasn't even in my vocabulary back then.

In *Elf*, Will Ferrell's character journeys to New York in order to find out who he is and what his place in the world is, but in reality the process is a little less exciting than that. When you begin on the road to true self-awareness, you just have to start walking, armed with a lot of patience, take a few tentative steps in a direction that you hope might be the correct one, see how it goes, find out how it will make you feel. Weeks and months of going nowhere, of experiencing little in the way of change may pass and it feels as though you are simply treading water and moving neither backwards nor forwards. And then you get a breakthrough.

Out of nowhere, you begin to see a new element of yourself coming to the fore, seeking its place in your world. After time, the jigsaw begins to look more complete, and eventually just the odd piece remains unfixed around the edges waiting to slot in somewhere.

Occasionally, a new situation arises and I feel unable to deal with it, not knowing whether to rely on the old me, or to try and find a different way of coping. It's a no man's land of emotions, a sensation of being lost in your own body. I do know how to get through these periods now though; I have finally learnt how to respond to the unknown – plod along, get your head down, and get on with it, run as much as possible, stay true to living without alcohol, and eventually the sun comes out again and shines on the answer, right in front of your face.

It's called self-discovery and it only begins to start fully when you stop drinking.

The Art of Resistance – December 11th 2012

I am currently in my twenty-first month without alcohol. I rarely feel the urge to go and get drunk, although I would be lying if I said that the thought had never entered my head during that time.

Usually as a result of being depressed, or something not going my way, or worrying about family or money, I have once or twice slipped into that mental place which is only a small step away from the wine aisle in Waitrose. It is a fleeting thought which maybe lasts a couple of minutes; the pros and cons are weighed up, I quickly come to realise that there are no pros because I play the movie to the end, and we all know how the movie finishes. To explain, 'playing the movie to the end' is simply a mental exercise which I use whenever I feel the urge for a drink. I picture myself with that first glass when all is going well. Then I fast-forward through the hours that follow and see myself moving on to another glass, finishing the bottle, opening a second – the end of the sequence always sees me drunk, and from there it's all cons. I know it will go exactly the way it went last time and in the long run I would lose: lose the knowledge that my children are happy and secure, my partner, my self-respect, my happiness, lots of money, any chance I have of regaining my figure after having a baby in my late thirties (I have discovered that the human body is not quite so resilient at 37 as it is at 23, which is when I had my first baby). In the end, I would always lose.

Those thoughts go at one hundred miles an hour, I take a sharp intake of breath and then begin to think how best to snap out of my mood, now that I have come to the realisation that booze isn't going to be involved in the process.

Before giving up alcohol, I would often experience these thoughts, instances of 'shall I, shan't I?' and the wine would always win. Even if I was on the wagon at the time, as soon as I had one of these moments I would give in to it and go and get drunk. I have since named these few seconds of internal conversation –a debate between the good and the bad, the devil and the angel – as 'Fuck It Moments.' And now that I am entering into my third calendar year of sobriety, I have developed an acute awareness of when I am suffering from such an attack on my state of mind and, where booze is concerned, I deal with it pretty well these days (if I do say so myself).

Fuck It Moments (FIMs?) do not just happen in relation to drink – I routinely experience FIMs when I am trying to lose weight, and this particular manifestation I have not mastered – yet. My weight is hovering around the 140 pound mark, and my pre-baby weight was about 132 pounds, so I really want to drop that last half a stone. I start off each morning with porridge, low-fat almond milk as a substitute for cows', some vitamins, juice; all going great.

I usually feel a little peckish around mid-morning but stave off the hunger pangs with a small banana and a glass of hot water with lemon. Oh, so virtuous, smug, and on the way to thin again until lunchtime, when, overwhelmed by hunger, I scoff a sandwich, apple, yoghurt, and three (count them, three!) chocolate biscuits. Oh God. I want to rewind, I feel a bit sick. I am thoroughly annoyed with myself.

What got me there? What led me to eat three chocolate biscuits? A colossal FIM, that's what. I opened the biscuit barrel, I stared down into the shiny wrappers, I knew that in that selection of bad boys lay a few thousand calories just waiting to latch on to my hips, and, after due consideration, I cast aside the lid, stuck my hand in, grabbed three, and said an almighty 'Fuck It'.

Such wayward behaviour is not going to lead me down

the path of slimness, back to my size ten jeans and the gorgeous dress I bought just a couple of weeks before I discovered I was pregnant and have only worn once. I know this, and I also knew (back in my drinking days) that every time I cracked open a bottle of wine I was heading for misery – maybe not on that night, but on a night to come, for sure, if I carried on. But I did it anyway, and continued to do so until I hit a large enough, nasty enough, frightening enough rock-bottom for me to successfully eliminate those alcohol FIMs from my life for good.

Now I need to do the same for the biscuit-tin FIMs. And I don't really want to hit three hundred pounds before I am so full of self-disgust that I never want to taste the sickly sweetness of chocolate ever again; I'd rather banish my biscuit FIMs quite a long way off that point.

More self-discovery, more alternative coping strategies, and more soul searching ... here we go again.

What Christmas Means to Me – December 13th 2012

It's that time of year again when everything goes slightly nuts and the world turns a little bit technicolor. Christmas can be overwhelming for many people, for a myriad of different reasons. Personally I have struggled with the festive period in the past because I was a single parent and had to share my daughter with her dad on Christmas Day, because I went wild in the drinks department (more than usual) and got even more hammered than my standard level of drunkenness, and because I suffered worse consequences as a result of being more sozzled than normal for much of the holidays.

Being drunk and then hungover, and having to deal with the associated mood swings in between, rendered me completely unable to be content with life's simple pleasures. I was forever searching for happiness, but was unable to find it when in the grip of alcohol. I therefore turned to increasingly inconsequential means in my efforts to locate that elusive state of mind; retail therapy when I had no need for new stuff (and could ill afford new stuff) romantic dalliances that kept me enthralled by their complicatedness and emotional rollercoaster turbulence, radical life changing decisions, the list goes on …

What I did not have when I regularly drank alcohol was an appreciation of the simple things in life or of what is truly of worth in our little worlds. I have spoken to many people who have quit drinking and who have since enjoyed similar moments of wonder at seemingly banal things; watching the rising sun, waking up feeling healthy and full of energy, seeing flowers in bloom bursting with colours never noticed before. What those people all have in common is the experiencing of an almost evangelical awakening in the weeks and months after ditching alcohol, when suddenly they are filled with a sense of clarity. Life becomes obvious; it all falls into place.

As time goes on this awareness grows stronger and stronger in me. I just know what I want, who I am and what life is all about. I understand me, I get it. And no time is it more prevalent than at Christmas when it can appear that all around you are losing their heads in a sea of alcohol.

For me, it has become wonderfully apparent that the next couple of weeks are about my two gorgeous girls having a special and happy time surrounded by their family who adore them, having more time than usual to spend with my other half, sharing delicious food and having a good laugh together. It's about appreciating everything that we have, remembering people who aren't so lucky, and trying to do something for them too.

That Was then and this Is Now – December 18th 2012

When I drank alcohol, this was my life: get up with a

hangover, slap on tons of make-up in an effort to disguise the fact, eat something fattening and carb-tastic for breakfast, not go for a run, stumble down to the park with the dog, hurry back home feeling slightly queasy, take daughter to school, catch bus to work feeling exhausted and a bit anxious, buy a large, full-fat latte and a cake for energy purposes, experience a sugar crash mid-morning due to fatigue, carb-loading, and sugar frenzy, drink more coffee, eat large and fattening sandwich with fizzy drink for lunch, drag myself through the afternoon, get home, eat an unhealthy dinner, stick the TV on, drink more wine to eradicate all of the above, and then slope off to bed feeling desperate for sleep.

Today I got up at 5 a.m. with a very poorly baby. She had some milk and then returned to her cot for an hour and a half while I did a monumental pile of ironing (multiple washes went on yesterday due to the baby being sick on an hourly basis) and made everyone's packed lunch. I took daughter number one to school, returned home and went for a long-ish walk with the baby and dog. Then I spent a couple of hours walking around the downstairs of the house with a crying baby over my shoulder, before eventually settling her after a dose of Calpol about 10.30 a.m. While she slept I crammed in about four hours' worth of work into one, before she woke up and we started walking about again for a further two hours.

Mum arrived as backup mid-afternoon, providing some alternative form of company to the little bundle of snot and tears (poor thing), and kept me company for a while. I then took the baby to the doctor's (viral, nothing he can do, just Calpol, fluids, sleep), brought her home and left her with Other Half while I went for a five-mile run, came back, cooked dinner, ate it, and then set about completing all the work that I didn't get done today.,

And during all of the pacing, consoling, cuddling, working and running that I ploughed through today, I never once felt tired, angry, impatient, or grumpy, and nor did I feel the urge to consume three times what I should in calorie intake, and nor did I consider for one second buying or drinking a bottle of wine to cope with my day. I just got on with it, like normal people do (with a bit of help from Grandma and OH).

I think that I am not bothered by booze any more. I think I am as I was intended to be, and it is such a relief.

If Tomorrow is the End ... (Tomorrow being 21/12/2012 when there was much chatter about the world meeting its maker) – December 20th 2012

If the world ends tomorrow, then I don't think I would be wracked with guilt and regret over mistakes and wrongdoings in my life. I have made mistakes, and too many to mention, but I feel that since giving up alcohol I have striven hard to iron out my creases (metaphorically speaking – the physical ones are all too apparent, a sorry sign of my diminishing youth), and for the most part have succeeded.

As a drinker, I would have told a very different story. There wasn't one aspect of myself that I felt fully happy about, not one characteristic that I genuinely felt proud of. I knew nothing of living life to the full and consistently fell short of my maximum potential, possessing the self-esteem of someone who persistently lives out her life in the shoes of a drunken, moody, instant-gratification-seeking narcissist. Not that I wish to be too hard on myself but that was me.

Addiction generally makes one self-serving and is a hard habit to break, much more difficult than resisting the demon drink. For months after I gave up, I would often be about to totally disregard someone's perspective or needs because they differed from mine, only to force myself to try a new method; self-sacrifice and a teeny bit of empathy. Over time I have rewired my brain and now I do think about consequences to a greater degree than merely how they will impact on me.

Learning not to be selfish breeds an altogether new phenomenon in the brain of the ex-addict; liking yourself, thinking you are OK, maybe even a nice person. And beginning to like yourself sets off a chemical reaction of its own – slowly, methodically, the building bricks of self-respect undergo a metamorphosis, from a scattered pile on the ground, to a solid, well-constructed wall, sturdy enough to weather a few storms. Once you have built your wall, you're all set – ready to face the world and all that it throws at you.

As someone who drank almost every night, mostly to excess, I had no walls, no defences to fight the fight with. Whenever something troublesome cropped up in my life, I drew on the old tried and tested (and routinely failed) methods of manipulation, crying, neediness, and ultimately giving up. I had no balls, no faith (I don't mean that in a religious way, but faith in a better life, faith in the sun coming up again, faith in finding the way out), and no gumption. I have all those things now (again, with the balls, I speak metaphorically).

So if tomorrow is the end for us all, I feel like I have done the best I could have done with the cards I got dealt. And you can't really do better than that.

Happy New Year! – December 30th 2012

I am not the party animal that I was in my youth. Long gone are the days when I would buy a ticket in October for an all-nighter New Year's bash, costing around £50, only to get completely out of it by about 11 p.m., thus never being able to recall whether or not I had actually enjoyed the night or not. I remember a few New Year's house parties which started out as brilliant occasions, full of friends, fun, and lots of alcohol, but all ended in some disaster or other (one springs to mind immediately, when a friend and I shaved off a male guest's fairly long hair at about 3 a.m. (with his consent, I add), only to show his new look off to his wife who proceeded to have a fit of the histrionics, accusing us of making her husband look as though he were going through chemotherapy. The whole party then joined in the slanging match for a good couple of hours, before everyone staggered home in the early morning light to sleep it off. (The husband wore a hat constantly for the next couple of months.)

The first New Year's Eve do that I went to as a drinker, aged somewhere in my mid-teens, I became the 'girl who cries at parties'. I have absolutely no idea as to what I was crying about, but do remember heaving over the toilet bowl for a while before finding some kind bloke who put his arm round me and attempted to force strong, black coffee down my throat. I remember nothing else. After sleeping it off, I awoke in the morning to find that I had inadvertently become the talk of the party, a strange girl (I had been invited by the two sisters who hosted the bash, but knew no one else there) who had spent hours on end gasping and dripping snot all over the shoulder of their mate who had kind of missed the party because of me. Apparently prior to that, I had also thrown a beer over some other bloke's head who tried to snog me under the mistletoe, but whose advances were not, it would seem, particularly sought after.

It will probably come as no surprise to you, then, when I tell you that I haven't bought a hot ticket for a posh do somewhere in town tomorrow night, but am instead staying at home with my girls. This is not because I no longer wish to socialise now that I no longer drink alcohol, but because from experience I know that many people view NY Eve as an occasion which warrants getting lashed, and I do hate being around people who are hammered.

So, in continuation of our little routine that we followed last year, my elder daughter (almost 14 and therefore this could potentially be the last New Year's Eve that she wishes to spend with her old mum) and I will be baking Nigella Lawson's chocolate orange cake, which is heaven on a plate and intended to serve about ten but easily polished off by two greedy girls enjoying their own private NY party. As that culinary delight bakes in the oven, we will get stuck into a load of beauty treatments; manicures, pedicures, facials, and cucumber slices on our eyes and laugh at some really awful celeb magazines. And then, cake semi-cooled but warm enough to still feature its *pièce de résistance*, the molten, gooey, utterly delectable chocolate orange centre, we will stick Jools Holland's Hootenanny on the TV and stuff our faces – marvellous.

This little party of ours also has the advantage of allowing for a meaningful New Year's Day, rather than one spent, as I have done frequently in the past, with the mother of all hangovers, periodically throwing up, and lying in a darkened room wishing that the train would stop running over my brain. I love the sentiment of the first day of a new year, a whole fresh 365 days, plain and untainted, free to do with whatever you choose, and so I value being with it sufficiently to enjoy it.

Seeing Is Believing – December 31st 2012

This morning I was on my way down to the park in the drizzly gloom, pram in front of me, and dog at my side. I was dressed in a beige puffer jacket, jeans and Uggs (I know, Uggs and rain is not a good mix but they are so warm I can't get them off my feet). The clothing is important – you'll see why in a sec. I stopped at the zebra crossing – large, brightly painted white and black stripes complete with two flashing yellow lights, one at either side, and was about to step on to the road when a car zoomed past, completely ignoring the pedestrian-friendly crossing.

I gesticulated, as you do, although mildly as I had the baby with me and I don't want to influence her gentle manner with my intolerance of bad driving, and then continued on my way across the road and on to the park. As I walked, I became aware of the sound of a car's engine to my left and looking across I saw the angry red face of the man who had just almost run me over. Winding down his window, he began to shout at me for not wearing brighter clothes (should I be equipped with a high-visibility jacket in order to safely negotiate a zebra crossing?). I was rather restrained in my response, although I did tell him off for being so aggressive.

He drove off and I embarked on an internal muttering for the duration of the fifteen-minute walk to my destination. Should I be wearing bright clothes? Should I have smiled at him as he almost took me, my baby, and the dog out in one fell swoop, hurtling along in his clapped-out Golf at forty-five miles per hour in a built-up area? Should I have given him more of a ticking off when he drew up alongside me and berated me for my beige clobber?

Half an hour later and I was just leaving the park when I looked up and saw two gentlemen in their seventies jogging along the pavement close to the park's entrance. 'How lovely,' thought I, 'that two men in their twilight years go jogging together. Not often you see that.' And then, as they neared me and I had a closer look, I saw that one of the men had no vision whatsoever and his friend was linking his arm through his blind companion's and steering him along a safe route.

This was a kind and wonderful thing for the friend to do, but I couldn't get over the massive amount of determination and fearlessness in the face of adversity demonstrated by the blind man. I was so impressed. If they had both had their sight I would have been impressed; given that one of them was putting all his trust and faith in his friend, and that they were both tackling disability and their mature years with such optimistic gusto, and doing it in the cold and the driving rain, I was nothing less than blown away.

I didn't give another thought to the arse with the bright red face, and was filled with a sense of all humanity being utterly fantastic all the way home.

Open Letter to Anyone Thinking of Giving up Booze this January – January 1st 2013

I'm thirty-seven years old and have struggled with depression, anxiety, and the odd panic attack throughout the last twenty years of my life. My nerves frequently got the better of me, and my obvious lack of confidence in work and social situations held me back and prevented me from fulfilling my potential for many years. If you had asked me to describe my personality a couple of years ago, I would have responded with a jumbled, insecure answer; unsure of who I really was, full of pretence as to the person I wanted to be, knowing that inside I didn't particularly like myself, but not fully realising how to change. All of that stopped when I quit drinking alcohol in April 2011.

If you have a sneaky suspicion that alcohol is controlling you a little more than you feel comfortable with then read on – this may be the first step you have subconsciously wanted to take for a long time.

If you binge-drink and subsequently get drunk a lot you will, whoever you are, occasionally make an idiot of yourself. You will say stupid things, have unnecessary arguments, fall over, lose your phone or handbag, text someone you really shouldn't, make sexual advances towards a person who is, how shall I put this …? Not quite at your usual standard. You may even put your safety at risk, walking home late at night alone, slightly wobbly, looking like an easy target for an attacker, or drink so much that you're sick after you have fallen asleep. Every time that you wake up the morning after a session where one or several of the above have occurred, your self-esteem will take a bit of a battering. Multiply those beatings by each weekend/night/day that you binge drink and you will appreciate that your self-respect and self-esteem are being severely and negatively affected by alcohol.

Alcohol depresses the central nervous system. Physiologically, that anxiety and nervy disposition that you, as a regular binge drinker, have probably noticed is increasing with age, is down to booze. When I drank, I had frequent panic attacks, the last one being so severe that I thought I was dying. I had to walk out of the packed cinema in which I was trying to watch *The King's Speech*, because I was fighting to breathe. It was hours until I regained my normal composure, and days until I fully recovered from the fright and trauma that I suffered as a result of thinking that I was on the way to meeting my maker. The reason behind this anxiety attack was that I had drunk too much beer the night before.

For years I pinballed between unsuitable relationships; one boyfriend would have the physical attributes I was looking for, but not the mental compatibility. I would dump the first one and jump straight in to another union with someone who had the brains and emotional energy I was after, but who, after time, I had no physical connection with whatsoever. I couldn't be alone. My depression and low self-esteem meant that I constantly needed the reassurance of being in a relationship just to feel wanted and loved. I was incapable of loving myself. Alcohol kept me from being in a happy and balanced relationship with a person who loves me as much as I love him.

Drinking put me in a perpetual state of either a) being drunk or b) being hungover. Neither of these conditions is conducive to a productive, fulfilling life. My career, financial wellbeing, and physical fitness were all below par (by a long way) when I drank. I am not a lazy person but I never achieved much during the years in which I got drunk. Since giving up drinking, my achievements just keep on growing each week – in turn this boosts my self-esteem and belief in what I am capable of. And so I keep on achieving and aiming higher.

Without drink in my life, my self-esteem has been restored; my anxiety and narcissistic tendencies have vanished, and guess what? I like myself! And the natural conclusion to that, of course, is that other people like me more too. I have finally found a man who I think is perfect (for me, at least), and we have a wonderful family life which I value above anything else. I am running regularly and have a 10k race (my second in three months) coming up at the end of February. My relationship with my elder daughter (at that tricky teenage stage) is great, and we are very close. I have bags of energy, and squeeze masses in to each and every day. I never stay in bed, idling away those precious hours that I could be spending on accomplishing something worthwhile. My skin and general appearance have improved, my eyes are bright, and I don't have to fight to keep a beer belly at bay. I am happy. The happiest I have ever been in my life, and this is down to one simple factor – I gave up booze.

House of the Flying Nappies – January 5th 2013

Do you ever wonder what your neighbours think about you? How they pigeon-hole you into a particular category or type? The thought crossed my mind a couple of hours ago when I opened the baby's window and flung a filled nappy sack out of the window to the ground below, a time-saving, odour-reducing technique that means the unwanted bag lands right next to the wheelie bin by the back door, and simultaneously ensures that it doesn't sit in the kitchen awaiting expulsion for several hours until somebody remembers it is there and does the necessary.

Anyway, as I closed the window, I noticed that the next-door neighbour was in her kitchen making a drink. She was standing by her window and must have seen the flying nappy sack as it zoomed past on its way to the bin. Then, a random thought popped into my head; are we known as 'House of the Flying Nappies'?

Do they think we are slightly nuts for hurling little plastic bags out of the bedroom window several times a day?

What else do they think of us?

We are quiet neighbours, I think – except for the baby's crying and that's excused as far as I'm concerned in the realm of neighbourly noise pollution because there is sod all that can be done about it. Our plastics bin is always overloaded, spewing empty milk bottles and yoghurt pots onto the ground around where it sits in the final days before the bin men dispose of its contents. The dog barks occasionally, but not to the point of distraction. We generally do not let her do a number two on the garden, so there are no unsightly dollops for our neighbours to see when they open their curtains. We don't have wild parties, tinker with old cars or motorbikes, play loud music, or have loud domestic arguments for all and sundry to hear. We are polite and friendly and exchange brief hellos if and when we bump into any of those who live in our immediate proximity.

Before I moved in here, I lived in an apartment with just my elder daughter. My neighbours there most likely had a very different impression of me. I quite often had people around, and we would stay up until 2 or 3 a.m. drinking, which subsequently meant periodically tottering outside to smoke fags, standing on the doorstep of the apartment block with wine glass in one hand and cigarette in the other (I should point out that these events generally happened when my daughter was at her dad's). I would frequently return home from a night out, utterly smashed, and stagger down the long, steep drive in high heels, and on more than the odd occasion I fell to the ground with a resounding smack, instigating some severe bruising.

One night in the winter, I took a particularly nasty tumble on some ice and proceeded to roll, commando-style, down a steep grass bank that was a slippery mix of slush, ice, and mud, landing embarrassed and covered in dirt in a heap at the bottom.

This drunken behaviour had the effect of turning me into an insecure, paranoid person with a nervous disposition. I would scuttle off, head down, if I spotted neighbours approaching me in the car park, terrified that they might have witnessed me inebriated and acting badly the previous night. Living on my own with a daughter as a woman in her mid-thirties, and clearly someone who enjoyed knocking back the vino on a regular basis, I am sure that my neighbours' opinions of me were less than sparkling.

I probably didn't help myself much when I routinely carried huge amounts of clanking empties across the car park to the communal bins, or if I was ever spotted walking home from the nearby supermarket, carrier bags full of wine bottles.

Considering the two categories: pissed-up old lush who smokes like a chimney and cannot converse with people in a normal, functioning way, or mum-of-two, resident of House of the Flying Nappies, who, in between looking after her kids, bloke, and dog goes jogging quite a lot and is often seen sitting at her laptop through the kitchen window, and whose blue bin gets a bit full from time to time, I definitely prefer the latter.

Learning from the Past – January 12th 2013

It is coming up to the tenth anniversary of my marriage ending. He walked out on me on Valentine's Day 2003, the day after I fell down the stairs and broke my foot. In the days leading up to his departure, I had absolutely no idea that my life was about to turn itself inside out, throwing me and all of my hopes and dreams for the future into utter disarray before dumping me in some awful no man's land where I would live out the next few years.

The actual act of him leaving plays out in my mind now, ten years on, as though it were a scene in a sub-average 1970s sitcom; me lying in the bed, plaster cast encasing my right leg up to the knee, him on his knees on the excessively deep deep-pile carpet, cramming his clothes into a suitcase before forcing the zip roughly in order to seal it shut; bewilderment on my face, dogged determination on his.

The following weeks and months meandered through bad to terrible to agonising pain, depression, with alcohol featuring prominently on the bleak landscape of my mental state. He stopped paying me money; I threatened to sell the family car. He moved in with a girlfriend and then criticised me for inviting a date back to the marital home in which he no longer lived. We fell into a childcare arrangement that would stick for the following decade, one which meant that he never came into the house to collect or drop off our daughter, but instead hung around at the bottom of the drive, engine running and an impatient look upon his face.

I felt as though I were carrying a neon sign around my person, one that flashed brightly the news to all who passed me that I was newly divorced, I couldn't keep my man, I was unwanted, a failure at life. The school playground was suddenly filled with laughing and joking married types, little nuclear families who embodied success and normality, and so I hung further and further back, desperately trying to fade into invisibility as I waited for my little girl to run out of the doors, some bright paper creation clasped in her hand that she had made that day.

When I look back now with ten years' additional life experience, the writing was emblazoned upon the wall that alcohol was about to become my best friend. With a complete disregard for my health and mental wellbeing, I hit the wine with a vicious desire to self-harm. Living through the emotional pain without anaesthetising it with alcohol was simply not an option. Wine crept in quietly through a back door that had been left slightly ajar, and proceeded to fill my whole existence with its far-reaching effects, becoming the unwanted visitor who outstayed its welcome and thrived on my continual downfall.

Ten years have brought with them immeasurable amounts of wisdom and self-awareness. If I could change anything, it would not be that my marriage had continued but that I had understood back then that drinking alcohol was only putting off the inevitable. As the wine flowed freely, the pain was not being washed away; rather it was redirected into a reservoir where it became concentrated and tainted, resting patiently for me to open the flood gates and let it free.

When I stopped drinking, the biggest mountain that I faced was tackling the previously ignored emotions that I had bottled up in the years following my divorce. I knew they were there, lurking in the depths of my consciousness and I dreaded the day when they would begin to trickle forth, forcing me to wet my toes in the painful aftermath of the hurt, betrayal, self-doubt, and anger that were born out of my marriage breakdown.

It's true that time heals, and when I regard my twenty-seven-year-old self floundering amidst a sea of alcohol and a refusal to acknowledge her feelings, I wish that I could whisper with complete assurance into her ear; 'it will all work out OK in the end'. I shouldn't have drunk as much as I did, but in all honesty I had no other way of coping at that time, and ultimately I came to the right conclusions. It did all work out OK in the end and the frayed edges got tidied up, the creases ironed out.

I learnt an awful lot from my divorce, and not a day passes by when I am not truly grateful for my current partner and my two daughters. When you lose the future that was yours, all mapped out in your head, organised and within your grasp, and you are faced with the task of building another one from scratch, it becomes impossible to live without gratitude for even the smallest thing.

The flurry of our lives spins along and carries us as though we were caught up in a whirlwind. When everything that you know disappears in an instant, you develop the ability to appreciate it fully and in the finest of detail when it finally comes back to you.

I'm so Sorry for Being Sober ... not! – January 23rd 2013

A recent topic of conversation on Soberistas.com has been about the embarrassment that some people feel regarding 'coming out' as a teetotaller, and it's something that I've been thinking about over the last few days, as a result. We live in a society that is heavily weighted in favour of alcohol as our preferred drug of choice, but also one that shuns those who are not 'able to handle it'. Those referred to as 'alcoholics' are often pitied, excluded, and frowned upon for their apparent weakness and inherent inability to just have a drink with the rest of us and not cause trouble, for themselves or for us.

It is similar for those who are overweight; we as a society tend to consider them at fault for not being able to just put the lid on the biscuit tin. It is fine for 'us' to indulge in pizzas and cakes, chips, and pasties because we know where to draw the line, but for those who continue to gorge themselves and who are subsequently obese, well, they have no one to blame but themselves.

Other drinkers are the drinks industry's best advertisers. Even a drinker who is on a short sabbatical due to antibiotics or pregnancy gets it in the ear as to why he or she is turning down an alcoholic beverage – 'Oh you poor thing, never mind – only nine months and then we can go out and get hammered again,' or 'Oh no, how long have you got to take them for? Ooh, two weeks without a beer – nightmare!'

Why? Why has it become so abhorrent to society in general that some of us may choose to live our lives fully present? Is it so ridiculous that, for some, their weekend may not revolve around stupidity, embarrassment, falling over, hangovers, and a multitude of regrettable incidents?

I remember how I viewed those who abstained from booze when I was a drinker. Killjoys, frumpy, boring, party-poopers; I would not have wanted to spend my time at a party or in the pub with teetotallers, simply because their presence would have highlighted my weakness, my addiction. I gravitated towards those who were equally happy getting sloshed and whose idea of fun was staggering around and talking rubbish.

Perhaps it is the case that, for heavy drinkers who are out to get pissed, teetotallers are their idea of the party guest from hell. But would we, as teetotallers, want to endure their company anyway? Listening to a boring, self-interested drunken idiot is my idea of hell – drunk people do not make good company to those who are with it enough to notice what they are talking about, and drunk people love being with other drunk people simply because it helps them to justify their own excessive drinking. And, of course, they are on the same wavelength: that is a very short, immature and inane one.

It is perhaps unrealistic to imagine that people who are stone cold sober and those who are absolutely out of it can get along together and have a merry old time. But then again, who would want to hang out with a heroin addict who had just shot up a load of top-whack smack? But there are plenty of people who drink alcohol who do not get completely off their heads and I do think, for them, it is inconsequential whether or not the person they are talking to is sober. And given the choice of the version of me drunk or sober, I know which one I would prefer to talk to (and it wouldn't be the one who was slurring her words, wobbling about, and flirting outrageously with every bloke in the room).

For every person who is brave enough to pour away the last bottle of wine and come to the healthy and happy choice to be sober, one more step is taken towards making teetotal living more normal, more acceptable. For every person who is strong enough to take a sober stand in this alcohol-fuelled society that we inhabit, we are building a viable alternative to the standard idea of 'a good time'. One day, in the not-too-distant future, I hope that it will be considered rather odd to head off to the pub on a Saturday night, spend a ton of money on a liquid that will annihilate your short-term memory, act in ways that you would never act when sober, and then as a result, waste your entire Sunday in bed with a hangover.

I Like not Drinking – January 26ᵗʰ 2012

For years I was scared of being sober. Then I stopped drinking.

Quite often, I am reminded of why I love my life without alcohol. Tonight was one of those nights. Here's why;

While out tonight, my thoughts were never controlled by anxieties about drinking alcohol. All I thought about was what was happening around me; I was fully present.

I'm going for a hard run tomorrow morning to compensate for the serious lack of it recently due to the snow. I haven't compromised my performance at all by drinking alcohol and I just know that tomorrow is going to be a great run.

My enjoyment of the evening was all real – I wasn't acting under the influence; it was really me.

I won't wake up tomorrow worrying about my health, something I said or that my daughter witnessed me while I was slightly drunk.

I got to come home and do a couple of jobs instead of letting them mount up for the morning. I know that I am 100% available for my sleeping baby should she wake up for anything.

I ate a gorgeous chocolate pudding that roughly equated to the calories in 3 big glasses of wine.

I remember getting home.

I had a great time!

When I go to bed, I can get stuck into the brilliant book that I'm reading.

I won't look tired/have a hangover/be sleep-deprived and grumpy when I get up in the morning.

What was I so scared about?

A Night to Remember – February 2nd 2012

We have just passed the 2nd anniversary of when I met my lovely fiancé.

I actually met him several months before the night when we finally got together, in the same pub. On both occasions I was rather the worse for wear but he, for some reason, was able to see right through my drunken demeanour to pinpoint the tiny promise of something unusual and precious – a soul mate. Don't ask me how, because my lasting memory of the first meeting we had was of me marching up to him in the street in order to state, in a very loud and slurred voice, that "I REALLY LIKE YOUR SMITHS T-SHIRT." The second time we met, I subtly revealed my attraction to him by fondling his thigh under the table as I sank large glasses of wine and smoked numerous cigarettes, blowing the smoke up into the dark air between us.

Not long after we met, I gave up drinking. This was down to a number of factors but largely because I had met the man who I wanted to have a happy time with, someone who I never wanted to hurt, and my soul mate, with whom I knew right from the beginning that I wanted to spend the rest of my life – minus the fog, recriminations, arguments, and regrets that result from drinking too much, too often.

Because of our ages and our mutual desire to have a baby, we got on with things pretty damn quick. I happened upon some old emails of ours last week, and read a thread that detailed our desire to get married approximately two weeks into our relationship. He proposed a couple of months later and we discovered the happy news that our daughter was on the way just a couple of months after that.

So, two years down the line and here we are; engaged, living in our house that we bought together, and our nine-month-old baby is sleeping upstairs in her cot. We didn't make much of a celebration of our anniversary last week due to heavy snow and a bad case of teething and associated nappy rash forcing us to cancel our planned night out, but you know what? It didn't seem like such a big deal and here's why:

Amongst the many errors of judgment that I made back in my drinking days, spotting my future fiancé in the middle of a pub car park and stumbling over to him to comment favourably on his T-shirt was not one of them; rather, it was one of my best moments. I think the T-shirt had a lot to do with it – in the same way that internet dating allows you to select potential partners by discovering their likes and dislikes prior to meeting in the flesh, so his wearing of a T-shirt emblazoned with one of my long-standing favourite bands of all time had the effect of revealing to me something of his character, i.e. that he has excellent taste in music, something which is of great importance to me.

So my impulsive, drunken behaviour for once did me a lot of good on the night of January 21st 2011. I found myself the most perfect man (for me) who has consistently made me happy, who is a fantastic dad to our baby and stepdad to my elder daughter, who believes in everything that I do (without being a kiss ass; and the former without the latter is an all-important trait), who looks after us all with kindness, patience, and understanding, and who is my best friend. I learnt how to be me and more importantly, how to like me, by being with him, and I learnt what it is to feel true contentment, because I never have to pretend to be something I'm not when he is around.

We missed a big night out for our anniversary but as my fiancé pointed out, it doesn't matter so much when you remember how many we have in front of us. Sean (if you are reading this) – happy belated anniversary and thank you.

Your Mind Is Your Instrument. Learn to Be its Master and not its Slave – February 7th 2013

I yearn for complete inner calm. I want to be one of those people who drift along with a look of serenity, a palpable sense of security about my being, an enviable ability to cope in even the most stressful of situations. Despite becoming more level-headed since ditching alcohol and with less of a tendency towards depressive or anxious episodes, I know there's still room for a deeper level of tranquillity.

I felt strangely at home as I entered the Kadampa

Buddhist Centre for my very first meditation class last Monday evening, despite never having being inside such a place before. After removing my shoes and coat I took my seat in the meditation room alongside about 30 others, and placed my feet on a cushion on the floor. It felt very normal to be sitting there in front of the Buddhist altar complete with numerous gold Buddhas and, bizarrely, a couple of large packets of tortilla chips (was Buddha a fan of crisps?).

We listened to our teacher's friendly introduction to the session and then jumped straight into a spot of meditating – I was a little taken aback at the speed with which we were getting to the nitty-gritty, but went with it regardless. I approached the idea of meditating with an open mind, and I believe that this is what enabled me to go pretty deep into a state of meditation almost immediately upon closing my eyes. This surprised me – past efforts at being hypnotised have failed miserably, largely owing to my somewhat cynical nature I think ... meditating was different, though, and it felt totally normal and right to be sitting amongst 30 strangers with my eyes closed, slowly drifting off into a state of mind rarely visited: serenity.

After half an hour, we were 'brought back into the room' and I was amazed that so long had passed – it felt closer to ten minutes. Our teacher then talked for a while about how, through meditation, it is possible to determine whether external events affect us in a positive or negative way, simply by becoming more in tune with our emotional energy. This is what I wanted to hear; I want that ability to shun the occasional burst of anxiety, the odd blue mood. I am deeply drawn to the idea that I call the shots with regard to my own emotions, and that I can develop an ability to see the positive in (almost) everything simply through practising this amazing art of meditation, which in itself is a powerful thing.

I can't remember feeling so relaxed ... EVER. I was so

chilled out that I was somewhat concerned about driving home. Visions of me swaying behind the wheel with an inane smile on my face as I ploughed straight through some red lights played in my mind's eye as I approached my car after the class. I was filled with a sense of positivity and love; I could not wait for the next class so that I could do it all over again.

Meditating just once has highlighted to me the extent that my lifestyle has come to represent the typically Western way of being; a life that is crammed full of activities, chores, and work, and one in which any spare time that I have is largely filled with checking emails, texts, or Twitter. I *never* sit and *just be*. No wonder I sometimes find it difficult to relax. Even when I go to bed I usually scroll through my tweets, or take a last look at my emails, when once upon a time I would always read a book.

Since the class I have made an effort to notice my emotions more, trying to pinpoint the stress points in order to better reverse the negativity. I have also become more aware of how I breathe, and have realised that I have a tendency to hold my breath when I become anxious, which in turn increases the anxiety only further. My aim now is to leave my phone downstairs when I go to bed, thus encouraging me to read and relax before trying to sleep, rather than scrolling endlessly through electronic messages of one type or another. I am also trying to find some time each day to practise meditating, although this is proving difficult with a nine-month-old baby, a teenager, and a dog to look after – I can see that it is possible but I need to attach a higher priority to it in order to fit it into each day.

And of course, I will be attending my meditation class next Monday.

Letting Go – February 10th 2013

The years I spent in between the end of my marriage and the start of my relationship with Mr Right (upstairs in bed) mostly took place in one district of Sheffield. In that area I lived in four different houses; two of them I owned, one I rented, and the other was an ex-partner's with whom I lived briefly before we split up and went our separate ways.

This area is stuck on the outskirts of Sheffield which means that I never have cause to pass through it and only go there if a specific reason arises (e.g. picking my elder daughter up from a friend's house, which I did last Thursday).

Anyway, I think I am reasonably happy at the moment; I'm in a good relationship – the best I've ever had – with someone I love very much, I have happily got on top of my booze dependency and I have two gorgeous daughters whom I love to bits. But as soon as I get close to this area of Sheffield where I lived through so much misery and heartache, I feel physically sick and can't wait to get out of there.

The houses were thrown up quickly around the time of the Industrial Revolution and are small and grey, built in a grid structure for speed and best use of space. The end result is a rabbit warren-like web of houses, their small, dark forms creating an air of claustrophobia and gloom.

Driving along the other night I was overwhelmed with a feeling of oppression and sadness, with each turning I made bringing home a whole bunch of bad memories and regrets. It made me realise that I kind of ran away from that place, making the physical break but never really dealing with the mental fallout of who I was when I lived there. I recognised that somewhere deep in my conscience there lurks a truckload of baggage which I need to deal with if I am to reach my goal of being truly at peace with myself, and I can only do that if I practise forgiveness of self.

The AA's 12-Step Programme includes the following steps;

• Made a searching and fearless moral inventory of ourselves.
• Admitted to God, to ourselves, and to another human being the exact nature of our wrongs.
• Were entirely ready to have God remove all these defects of character.
• Humbly asked Him to remove our shortcomings.
• Made a list of all persons we had harmed, and became willing to make amends to them all.
• Made direct amends to such people wherever possible, except when to do so would injure them or others.
• Continued to take personal inventory and when we were wrong promptly admitted it.

I'm an atheist and not massively drawn to the AA as a strategy for conquering a dependency upon alcohol (not to say that I disagree with the AA, but I don't feel that it's a good fit for me), and therefore these God-related points are not something that I can really attempt to adhere to. *But* I can see the benefit of trying to come to terms with how we've behaved when under the influence – of moving forward with a sense of having resolved past grievances and healing old sorrows.

I find it very difficult to distance myself from the past when I am in that area of Sheffield, my home during my darkest years. For several days after being in that area, old, unwanted memories linger like the unpleasant smell of rotting vegetables hiding undetected at the back of a fridge. I don't need God or anyone else to humbly remove my shortcomings or to remove the defective aspects of my character – I've done that bit by myself, thank you very much (well, it's a work in progress but I'm getting there). It's the past that I cannot let go of, but until I do, I know I will always be able to taste that tang of restlessness – unease, with a few concentrated drops of shame in the mix.

Here then lies a new challenge in my search for serenity and happiness in 2013 – to finally let go of those miserable years and to accept that everyone makes mistakes – the important thing is to learn from them and not repeat them (too often!). Learning to let go of past mistakes is an important part of self-growth – rather than it being an exercise in letting yourself off the hook, forgiveness of self is actually a positive way to learn to forgive others, and to create a more peaceful existence for your future self. Acknowledge your past errors, apologise to yourself and make a promise that you won't walk that path again. And remember:

Forgiveness of self is impossible until you stop longing for a better past.

The kindest and most compassionate thing you can do for yourself and for others is to forgive yourself.

You are still mortal and therefore you are going to make mistakes.

My final and favourite quote on this topic:

"We are made wise not by the recollection of our past, but by the responsibility of our future."
George Bernard Shaw

Out with the Negative; in with the Happy! – February 20th 2013

As a child I perpetually lived in the moment. I was lucky enough to have a very happy childhood, one that was full of Enid Blyton-esque adventures in sunny fields with friends, roller-skating up and down the cul-de-sac that I grew up on, baking cakes and biscuits, reading and writing voraciously and never seemingly worrying about anything, past or present. I just was.

During the years that I spent drinking heavily, my state of being was at the polar opposite of those younger halcyon years. Anxiety levels were astronomical, with worries over relationships, divorce settlements, my daughter's wellbeing, how much I was drinking, paying the bills, whether I was causing my body untold harm through all those cigarettes and bottles of wine ... my mind seemed to be set in a constant whirring mode, churning and cogitating and over-thinking all these troubles that in the end, were what they were; none of the excess pondering made the slightest dent in any of it. The outcomes were the same regardless.

Nowadays I experience 'normal' worries. A small amount of worrying does us good and if we existed in a blissful childhood state, skipping about without a care in the world, we would find our little lives running to a standstill fairly quickly. Normal worrying helps us keep a rein on our budget, encourage our children to work a little harder on their homework when they begin to spend too much time on Facebook, put a bit more effort into our relationships if we feel they are not as tight as they perhaps might be.

A huge difference that I have noticed in the last few weeks since I began to practise the art of meditation is that I seem to be able to control better those uncontrollable fits of anxiety, the ones that render you feeling sick and with palpitations – a bit like the way I felt yesterday morning on my way to the ITV studio to appear on *Daybreak*. I caught myself becoming overwhelmed with fear in the back of the car as we travelled past the London Eye, looming out of the early dawn with its blue-lit cars suspended over the Thames, my stomach churning and my mind rattling along at a hundred miles an hour. Then I made a decision to not feel that way.

Hang on a minute! It's my mind, I call the shots.

I took some deep breaths, focussed my mind, and cleared my thoughts. I began to consider that this experience was something to be savoured – it's not every day that you get to go on live TV and sit next to Dr Hilary! I recalled how this would have been dealt with by me as a child – I would have seen the whole journey through eyes wild with excitement, from arriving in London late at night, staying in a nice hotel, being picked up by a car with tinted windows and taken to ITV's studios ... I would have loved every minute thirty years ago. Instead, I had been allowing my out-of-control worrying to ruin the whole event.

Practising meditation has allowed me to be much more aware of negative thinking patterns and has also taught me that I don't have to accept them – I can decide whether I perceive something in a positive way or a negative way. Yesterday I chose to see things positively, and I found myself enjoying the whole experience; by simply altering the way I decide to process external situations, I have also made myself a little bit braver and next time (if there is a next time) I will approach things in a far more relaxed fashion, right from the off.

Only you can determine whether you tackle things positively or negatively – taking the former option makes life a million times easier and more enjoyable!

Drinking/not Drinking – February 23rd 2013

Why did you used to drink so much?

Because I thought it was a fast-track route to forgetting stuff and relaxing.

Why didn't you just stop when you'd had enough?

I couldn't – when I drink, my brain doesn't compute the fact that I should stop when I've had enough; instead, my desire to drink went into overdrive and it became all I cared about.

Are you an alcoholic?

I used to be addicted to a substance that alters my behaviour and mood, and which I craved on certain occasions because I misguidedly believed that it would help me get through a given situation. Since I stopped drinking, I never have those thoughts any more as I am now fully aware of the fact that my body and mind operate at their optimum when they aren't subjected to alcohol.

Is it difficult being teetotal?

I am more aware of the fact that we live in an alcohol-mad culture than I was when I drank. As a drinker you slot into the norm, but when you give it up you become part of the minority. That bothered me at first but now I feel very proud of being teetotal and I wouldn't want to drink alcohol, even if I knew that I could drink it without all the negativity that occurred as a consequence back in my boozy days.

What are the benefits of not drinking?

I could say that the benefits are more energy, better sleep, easy weight management, brighter eyes, clear skin, even moods, no depression, and no anxiety – they are all fantastic and valid benefits to be found from giving up the booze. But the really amazing thing is that I have discovered who I am; I didn't need to go on a six-month trek round India to find myself; I just had to put down the bottle. I love the world and my life, I care about my surroundings, and I'm passionate about things outside of my immediate goings-on. I have remembered how to engage properly with people and how to love others with my whole heart, instead of just the bit that isn't thinking about alcohol.

Giving up alcohol has given me back my mind. That's the best thing about it.

I Choose – February 26th 2013

When I stopped drinking alcohol, I acknowledge that I spent a few weeks, if not months, in recovery. By this I mean that I invested a fair bit of energy in dealing with a newly discovered concept – emotions. Previously, I had poured vast amounts of pinot grigio or chardonnay down my throat whenever I split up with a boyfriend, was not successful in a job interview/promotion, got rained on, received a large and unexpected bill, graduated, had a birthday, received some surprising and happy news, and so on … basically, I was not accustomed to listening to my feelings and subsequently I was not familiar with acting upon them in a positive and helpful way.

It wasn't particularly pleasant at times, all that 'getting to know myself' stuff, and there were many occasions when I felt like throwing the towel in, marching up the road to my local and getting stuck into a nice bottle of their finest dry white and a packet of 20 cigarettes. But I didn't.

A little voice inside, quiet but impossible to ignore, told me that if I gave in now I would be undoing all of my good work and propelling myself back to square one, where I would have to begin the whole sorry business of 'recovery' once again. And so I persevered.

After several months I stopped experiencing any negative thoughts about living alcohol-free and instead adopted a thoroughly different mindset; one which made me see that I am, in fact, a chooser – and being someone who has the freedom to choose a lifestyle that is so positive and good for the soul is an empowering and wonderful thing. At that point, I ceased to regard myself as being 'in recovery' and realised that I was *recovered* and could now get on with the business of living.

I will always be a person who cannot simply have 'one for the road' or 'a sneaky tea-time pint' – for me alcohol was, and for ever will be, an all-or-nothing substance. But I most certainly do not consider that this makes me an alcoholic for ever, or in recovery for ever – not at all. I made a choice to stop drinking, and I continue to practise that choice every day because I am *a chooser*. This is what I choose:

I choose to wake up energised and with no regrets every morning.

I choose to be the best parent I can be without ever jeopardising my children's safety or emotional security.

I choose to invest all my time and energy into worthwhile people, projects, and activities.

I choose to maintain a good level of health and physical fitness, thus optimising my chances of not dying prematurely of cancer, liver failure, or heart disease.

I choose to spend my money on things that I need and which add value to my life or to that of my family's.

I choose to not poison my body with toxins that depress my central nervous system, making me anxious and prone to dark moods.

I choose to not spend hours of each week agonising over whether or not I can have a drink of alcohol or not.

I choose to get to know myself, free of any external and false influences – I give myself the chance to be me.

I choose not to ingest mind-altering substances that make me say or do things that I will regret and which will fill me with shame and self-hatred.

I choose to give myself the best possible chance at happiness.

Sick of Booze – March 1ˢᵗ 2013

I have been ill this week for the first time in ages. Off the back of the baby's two-week battle with sickness, cold, and raging temperatures (she is now recovered), the rest of the family have subsequently been struck down with aches and pains and noses that are constantly running.

I had forgotten what it feels like to be ill, and have been reminded of how awful I used to feel back in the booze era, on an almost daily basis, as I struggled to pretend that I didn't have a hangover. This week, everything has been difficult, from sleeping (nose stuffed up and unable to breathe properly), to eating (feel constantly sick and not even Cadbury's Creme Eggs are doing it for me), to walking the dog and cooking dinner. Being ill is rubbish!

I haven't had the energy or motivation to do anything other than collapsing on the settee after the baby has (eventually) gone to sleep and all the chores have been done.

The last few days have served to remind me, however, that one of the greatest gifts that living alcohol-free gives us is feeling energetic and full of health, and that even when we're struck down with a genuine illness our bodies are better able to fight it due to not being subjected to excessive amounts of alcohol on a daily basis. I did used to feel somewhat justified in drinking some 'medicinal' wine in the old days whenever I was ill; snuggling up on the settee and cracking a bottle of rioja seemed entirely reasonable and a positive way to combat whatever illness I was suffering. Bonkers!

Instead, I have been drinking lots of hot water and lemon, sucking Strepsils, and sleeping as much as is possible when one has a ten-month-old baby (and an ill one at that) to look after. Being sensible and doing the right things for your body when it is not one hundred per cent healthy feels a hell of a lot better than smoking and drinking wine ever did, in some sort of bizarre, denial-fuelled bid to be a true rebel.

When the baby wakes up, I'm going to take her out to buy her some new toys – a little treat for her after such a rotten fortnight, which included a trip to the Children's Hospital for a super-high temperature. That money would have gone on wine and cigarettes once upon a time … oh, how I love my life as a non-drinker – even with a horrid cold to contend with! Life is definitely better *sans* booze.

The 4 Emotional Stages of Sobriety – March 4th 2013

When I stopped drinking in April 2011, I embarked on a journey that began in the early hours of one spring morning and which has taken me on a convoluted and emotionally turbulent ride, finally allowing me to climb off into a place that resembles contentment and emotional stability. For anyone who has recently ditched alcohol, I have written the following; it outlines my experiences of the different emotional stages I travelled through in the 23 months between my last drink and today, and I hope that it might help those of you who are new to sobriety by giving you a bit of a heads-up of what to expect in this new and exciting chapter of your life.

Stage 1 – The joys of the natural high

As an alcohol-dependent person who had felt terribly out of control of her own life for many, many years, the first few weeks and months of living as a non-drinker were a breath of fresh air. The joy of waking up each day and not immediately running through a mental checklist of who I had insulted/let down/hurt the night before was beyond compare. I literally jumped out of bed in the mornings, a massive weight of anxiety removed from around my neck. Gone were the fears of developing breast cancer or dying of liver failure; the dreaded guilt and shame that I suffered as a result of doing something stupid and/or irresponsible when under the influence were gone – I felt free as a bird. Going out socially was a wonderful experience, as previously I had always felt butterflies in my stomach as I feared how the night ahead would unfold, never knowing how drunk I would get and where that state of mind would take me. Instead I knew that I was finally calling the shots – I would decide who to talk to, what I said, whether or not I chatted someone up/allowed myself to be chatted up; this was me, and not that idiot who I became after too much wine. This first period was characterised by a sense of freedom, lightness, and joy.

Stage 2 – Boredom and why me?

OK, nothing lasts for ever. After a couple of months, I became beset by a black mood and the doubts began to creep in. The little devil on my shoulder grew in his boldness and whereas the angel had definitely ruled the roost in the early weeks, the voice of addiction became louder and more assertive in this second phase. The following are examples of the conversations I had with my devil: what if I'm not addicted to alcohol? What if I just need to learn how to moderate? Could it be that my boyfriend would prefer me to be more under control to suit him better, and that's why he professes concern at how much I was drinking?

Then the devil would start talking. Who is he to think he can control you? Doesn't he see that you're a free spirit – you don't run with the crowds, you are different, untamed; alcohol is a part of who you are. Everyone else in the world is allowed to drink and get drunk – why the hell can't you? It's not fair.

In the midst of this period, I initiated a blazing row with my boyfriend (now my fiancé) and told him in no uncertain terms that I was planning on drinking that night. He tried in vain to convince me that it was the addiction talking, but how could it be? It was so convincing and powerful – that was me talking, the voice was coming right from within me. We stormed up to the pub together and he ordered himself a pint and sat outside. I scuttled up to the bar after he had taken his seat, my heart beating ferociously and my cheeks burning.

I ordered a lime and soda.

Every tiny piece of me wanted to buy alcohol except for the tiniest voice, hidden somewhere deep inside me. It told me that I would never change if I bought a glass of wine now; this moment was definitive – it would determine whether I stayed on the road to self-discovery and a better life, or whether I returned hell for leather to that old path of destruction. I couldn't let myself down, and I stuck to my guns.

Stage 3 – Resolute but bitter

I turned a corner that night and all doubt was removed. The devil fell away from my shoulder, but nothing replaced him for a long time. There followed months of falling in a vacuum; I accepted my lot as a non-drinker but I wasn't happy about it. I missed alcohol terribly – I wanted to sit outside pubs in the summer, laughing gaily over a large glass of icy-cold white wine. I wanted to get glammed up and drink cocktails in a fancy bar, enjoying the sense of relaxation, of throwing caution to the wind and forgetting my cares for a night. At times, I hated other people for being 'allowed' to drink. This was a very difficult stage.

After several months of this, I read Jason Vale's book, 'How to Kick the Drink … Easily!' and my life changed. I suddenly saw alcohol for what it really is, and I knew that all those voices and cravings I had felt over the last year or so were as a result of slowly weaning myself off a very powerful and prevalent, socially acceptable drug. I gave myself a break – began to let go of the regrets and shame that I was still carrying around with me. The bitterness slowly dissolved into contentment; the sun began to shine once again.

Stage 4 – Understanding me as a non-drinker

The final stage is the best. Over the last couple of years I have worked through many emotions and feelings of regret, sadness, anger, bitterness, sorrow, remorse, jealousy, and fear. After a good year and a half, the negativity became noticeably reduced; as my self-esteem grew and my appreciation of the world and everything in it was heightened due to the clarity that comes from not poisoning your body with alcohol on an almost daily basis, it was as though the bad thoughts were mopped up one by one by my new-found positivity and optimistic take on life.

I stopped experiencing wine envy when I walked past a pub full to bursting with drunken, loud revellers, but I didn't huff and puff either – drinking is their choice, just as not drinking is mine. I love my life and I am grateful every day that alcohol no longer plays a part in it. I never have moments on a Friday night like the ones I had in the early days – DVD, nice bottle of wine, oh how wonderful it would feel to just kick back and slowly feel the alcohol ameliorating all my anxieties. It simply isn't a part of my consciousness any more – I drove it out and replaced my addiction with happiness and good health.

It would have been perhaps easier to jump straight from Stage 1 to Stage 4, but the journey has allowed me to learn so much about who I really am, minus the veneer of alcohol, and I wouldn't have missed it out even if I could have. I had no idea that when I stopped drinking it would be necessary to undergo such emotional turbulence; to feel as though my old self has been through a seriously intense recalibration before being reinstalled with a new lease of life, eventually leaving a turbocharged version of me back in the driving seat of my future. I didn't expect any of that, but I am one hundred per cent happy that it happened.

Working 9 to 5 – March 6th 2013

Today I wanted to share with you a great example of how the mind works better without the fog of alcohol sullying its functionality. Tomorrow I return to work after twelve months maternity leave has allowed me to enjoy every waking moment with my gorgeous baby girl, watching her grow and develop into a little personality from those early days of her being a tiny, red-faced, milk-guzzling machine.

My thoughts on returning to work have not all been positive, if I'm honest. For many months, the notion of having a paid job simply disappeared off my radar, and my daily routine gradually evolved into a series of walks in the park, household chores, meeting friends for coffee, playing with the baby, oh yes, and setting up Soberistas! A couple of months ago, I experienced the vaguest of recollections of what it is to actually go into an office, carry out a job, interact with colleagues, and attend meetings, but swiftly pushed it to the back of my mind, telling myself that it was still a long way off in the future.

This week, the startling reality of having to say goodbye to my little baby at 8 a.m. and to not see her little cherubic face until 5 p.m. hit me in the face like a large sack of bricks. I spent a day in tears. The childlike element of my persona (which lay behind the manipulative behaviour and occasional tantrum of years gone by, and which was often brought to the fore after drinking heavily) returned for a brief period. I wanted someone to resolve this issue, to somehow enable me to stay at home with my baby and never have to leave her in someone else's care.

Here is the difference between the mind of someone who drinks regularly, and that of a sober person; I worked through the feelings; I rationalised it out in my head; I had a conversation with myself and with those closest to me and I weighed up the pros and cons. After a couple of days of that, I came to the following conclusions – most people have to work in order to cover their overheads – why should I be exempt; the money will pay for extras like holidays and horse-riding lessons for my elder daughter; my baby will learn to interact with other people than her immediate family, thus allowing her to develop her social skills; I will interact with people outside of my current existence which mainly comprises of other mums and their babies. I will value even more the time that I spend with my family when I get home from work; and, finally, on the days that I work, the dog will be getting an hour-long walk with a pack of dogs and her new dog walker, which will add excitement and pleasure to her little life.

So, a couple of days to mull things over and I have come up with a myriad of reasons why my return to work is a *good thing* (and it warranted some new clothes, which is an extra bonus!) Compare that with the old me, who would have dealt with the same situation by necking a few bottles of wine, fuelling my burgeoning depression and preventing me from thinking clearly, and ultimately causing me to perceive my return to work as nothing but a big bunch of awfulness – which it would have then become, in a self-fulfilling-prophecy-type manifestation.

Positivity is most definitely the easiest and best path to choose in life.

Happy Mother's Day – March 9th 2013

I've said it before, and I'll say it again; life without alcohol means living a life that's anchored in reality, rather than chasing the promise of the carefree and extraordinary pleasures that alcohol dangles but never delivers.

The reason I am reminded of this tonight is because it's Mother's Day tomorrow. In days gone by, I would have been eagerly anticipating this occasion because somewhere amidst the cup of tea in bed, the hand-made card, the thoughtful gift, and the sudden and out of character display of help around the house, would have been the beckoning finger of several large glasses of wine.

It might have been a meal booked in a restaurant, or friends or family invited round to the house for a Sunday roast, but however the celebration manifested itself, wine would have been on the cards.

The first glass would have been the appetiser, a taste of

things to come. After half a bottle had gone, the nervousness would have begun – how long can I make that last for? Would it be terrible to crack a second bottle before we've reached 3 p.m.? Feeling slightly drunk and the meal is going to pot … would it be OK to just kick back and get drunk for the rest of the day?

The present and the hand-made card would drift into a distant memory; the day would lose its meaning and become a lazy, hazy afternoon marred by the effects of the crisp, cold liquid poured into the glasses like a tinkling fountain constantly flowing until bedtime.

Thank God those days have entered into the history books. Thank God the person who did that has woken up to reality and seen the damage that those apparently innocuous and fun Sundays did to those around her. Thank God the person who drank alcohol in such a reckless fashion will be having a very different day on Mother's Day, 2013.

This mum will be getting up with the baby at 6 a.m., because she can't think of anything she would rather do than see that happy little face smiling from the cot at first light. This mum will be going to the gym with her elder daughter later in the morning for a swim and a coffee, and then spending the afternoon with her wonderful family, eating, laughing, and chatting. The day will be real. There will be no recriminations, arguments, or regrets. There will be no addiction looming in the mind of this mum, nothing to steal a single thought away from real life.

Tomorrow is Mother's Day and it's about mothers, and nothing else.

Practice Makes Permanent – March 16th 2013

It is inevitable that when you first cut alcohol out of your life, you will have the odd or perhaps intensely frequent craving for a drink, depending on your level of addiction and consumption. These thought processes will eventually diminish over time but it is important to remember at the outset that our brains need a fairly substantial length of time to become rewired.

Neurological pathways lie behind our habits, the neuroplasticity of our grey matter meaning we are forever responding to life experiences by the physiological altering of our brains' structure and function, which in turn affects the habits we employ and our general behaviour. In simple terms, the more you tread a particular path of your neural network, the stronger and more apparently 'natural' the associated behaviour will become.

'Practice makes perfect' is not simply a throwaway maxim – it is neurological fact.

Breaking a long-standing habit or addiction can take a long time, which can be frustrating and ultimately self-defeating. As the weeks drag by and you find yourself experiencing longing and desirous thoughts about the cold, crisp taste of chardonnay on a summer's evening, it can feel as though you will never successfully move forward and think differently. But you will – eventually.

The key is to stick with your intention through thick and thin; in order to rewire your brain, you *must* begin to walk new pathways in your neural network. At first, those paths will be difficult to manoeuvre, thick with brambles and weeds, but over time you will squash the vegetation flat with the weight of your steps and a small but distinctive passage will begin to emerge. Follow that route a while longer and the path will become marked, a natural road to choose. The old alleyways that led you to destruction and misery will gradually witness the dawning and then the maturity of prickly undergrowth, making them inaccessible.

With time, you will automatically opt for the easy route – the gently winding walkway, bathed in sunlight and filled with the sound of happiness, will override the erstwhile dominant negative roads to destruction and loss of self. Stick with it, stay firm – practice makes permanent.

Last Night I Dreamt – March 19th 2013

I threw myself into a sober challenge last night – I went to watch Johnny Marr, former guitarist of The Smiths, play at Sheffield's Leadmill.

In the past, this would have been all about the alcohol but now, obviously, that is not who I am and so it did not form an integral part (or any part) of the evening's unfolding.

I wanted to report back to you on a truly amazing experience. First off, the Leadmill is a venue that I have frequented on countless nights out, and prior to last night I have always been the worse for wear upon arrival. Looking round while sober was a strange experience – as though I recognised it but only out of a dream; semi-formed memories came back to me, rolling back and forth like a lazy tide.

People everywhere clutched beer in plastic pint pots, there was me, standing amongst a sea of alcohol and anticipation for the arrival of a guitar legend, with a glass of Coke, ice, and a slice.

Something that struck me hard last night about being there to see Johnny Marr is that, in giving up alcohol, I haven't lost me; the Lucy that poured booze down her neck on some misguided rock 'n' roll mission, smoking like a chimney and gradually slipping into inebriation as the night wore on, well, she was not present. But the real, human, character of me, the part of me that loves watching amazing, world-changing musicians like Marr live on stage, the part of me that soaks up the atmosphere and has the ability to lose herself in the music, to step away from the stresses and busyness of everyday life for a couple of hours, eyes glued on the stage, not wanting to miss a second of what proved to be an incredible performance; she was right there.

Being sober just made it better; there was no fogging of the senses, no wobbling, no over-thinking about how to get more alcohol when you're stuck fast in the middle of a heaving crowd, fastened together so tight that the hundreds have become just one seething mass of bodies.

I just listened and watched.

And Johnny Marr did indeed fill the shoes that the teenage Smiths-idolising Lucy had placed him in over twenty years ago. With a mix of new stuff from his album, *The Messenger*, and old Smiths classics ('There is a Light That Never Goes Out', 'Stop Me if You Think You've Heard This One Before') Marr consistently delivered to a mixed crowd of old diehards and younger fans. His guitar-playing was as effortless and mind-blowing as it ever was – for me, seeing him perform without Morrissey by his side only served to highlight his musical genius even more, elevating his new material to become one of my current favourite albums.

I owned sobriety last night; I concentrated on what I was there to see. My brain wasn't dulled, my motives for being there not lost to a pointless addiction. I revelled in being present; I felt as high as a kite, full of meaning and anchored to what matters to me in my life. Last night, one hundred per cent of me got a massive kick out of living, of beating my problems and loving the present.

Moments of Weakness – March 26th 2013

There's something in the way my (everyone's?) brain works that means that I have a strong propensity to lie to myself. Well, not so much lie as choose to ignore; to remain in denial, avoiding opening the blinds completely in an effort to hide away in the shadows of what I know, staying tucked away in my comfort zone.

I used to do this with regards to wine – at night I would lie in bed feeling for lumps as evidence of tumours, so convinced was I that I had developed cancer as a result of my wayward lifestyle. In the mornings, I would stare at my haggard reflection, the dark circles below my eyes and magnified pores of the skin on my face, the flushed cheeks that had nothing to thank blusher for. I would berate myself for being an irresponsible mother, a less-than-perfect girlfriend.

And then, by about 5 p.m., there I would be, having a perfectly reasonable little chat with myself which would, absolutely guaranteed, end in a drive to the supermarket for a bottle of cold pinot grigio, perhaps a chablis if I needed to feel as though I were 'treating' myself, and the merry-go-round would begin again.

The fact was that the health anxieties I was experiencing, the sorry-looking reflection in the mirror, the urge to overeat carbs each morning owing to consistent, nagging hangovers, they were all factors that resulted from drinking alcohol and nothing else; the simple truth was that if I had just stopped drinking, all of the negativity in my life would have vanished – which, I am pleased to say, in the end it did.

The reason I am writing this today is because it occurred to me over the weekend that I am now doing exactly the same thing with my weight. OK, I'm not overweight, but I would like to lose about half a stone in order to reach my ideal size. Because I don't drink and I run regularly, I do maintain a good weight for my height, but I know that the reason those last few pounds won't budge is because I give in to that voice in my head that tells me that the chocolate bars (yes, plural) I eat after dinner, or the pizza we order in on a busy night when cooking a meal somehow seems to fall by the wayside, aren't really that bad, the voice that tells me that those extra five or six hundred calories a day aren't really going to make a difference.

Well, guess what? They do. They are the difference, just as that bottle of wine, so easily scooped up off the shelf in Waitrose and plonked down amongst the bread, yoghurts, and tins of baked beans, was the difference between what I was then, and what I am today.

It's a moment of weakness, of denial, and the efforts to achieve your goal just vanish into the air like a puff of smoke as if they never existed in the first place. This is why I'm going to try making some visual reminders of my goals.

Writing the reasons why you want to lose weight or give up booze down on pieces of paper and sticking them all over the kitchen, or wherever you feel your trigger points are most likely to occur (in your purse maybe, so you catch a glimpse of it just before you go to pay for that bottle of wine you've picked up on the way home from work), is one idea. Keeping a food/booze diary is another, or sticking a picture of yourself at your ideal weight up on the bathroom mirror … Keep a list of all the reasons why you hated yourself so much the morning after your last binge, and read it nightly so that you don't forget.

My weakness now is chocolate – I'm pretty healthy in every other respect, but I know that my weight will continue to bug me if I don't manage to lose those last few pounds. So today, I will put some of the above strategies into practice and hope that some/all of them work.

Sliding Doors – March 30th 2013

Do you ever wonder where your life may have taken you had you made different decisions? For me, a large element of learning to let go of my past mistakes has been the understanding and acceptance of who I am today, and how all the choices I have made on my journey to this point have amalgamated to create who I have become.

I have had relationships which would, I'm sure, have taken me to very different places had I remained in them; the boyfriend whom I moved to London to live with in my early twenties was an ardent socialite, a lover of debauchery, and not someone I could imagine I would ever have become sober while involved with. My ex-husband, the workaholic, whom I erroneously believed to be the love of my life prior to him walking out and leaving me with a broken foot, crutches, our four-year-old daughter, and a mad puppy on Valentine's Day 2003, would only have stunted my emotional and personal development had we remained married, and I am eternally grateful that he left me as he did.

The years that followed his leaving were admittedly awful, the wine drunk in far too vast quantity, but the ensuing depression and dark days were, I believe, all vital ingredients in building my emotional strength and character. If he had stayed, I am certain that I would never have grown as a person, would never have fought and beaten my demons, and ultimately, never have drunk so much that I then considered it absolutely essential that I conquered my alcohol dependency.

In the years that followed my divorce, I had relationships with a few men, all of whom were lovely in their own way but none of whom would have helped me find the road to sobriety, self-discovery, and finally, learning to like myself. They were all heavy drinkers, and despite their collective disapproval of the multifarious displays of my terrible drunken behaviour, none were brave enough to take on the dragon that was Lucy's beloved bottle of wine. Had I stayed with any one of those partners, I probably would have drunk myself into an early grave.

In the midst of all that pinballing from one bad relationship to another, the mornings of self-hatred that evolved into afternoons in the pub and evenings of comatose drunkenness, arguments, and hour upon hour of wasted life, the smallest desire to escape my situation began to gain momentum. So insignificant that I didn't even know it was there for a long time, the seed that grew into a very real knowledge that I must stop drinking took years to establish itself. The boyfriends who were a mistake, the under-achieving at work due to constant hangovers, the inability to move forward in my life, and the associated frustrations that arose as a result, gradually amassed to provide the food and water required to nurture my growing awareness.

And one day, there it was – it turns out that all those bad choices were not so bad after all, because in the small hours of a Thursday morning almost two years ago, I woke up and realised that the seed had become a tree. All of a sudden, I recognised how I should be spending my life, and I began to live it. If none of my bad times had happened, if the years of pain and grimness had been erased and left me with nothing but an easy ride, I wouldn't be here, doing this. No contentment, no new baby, no self-esteem, no Soberistas, no gratitude for my life.

There will always be sunshine after the rain.

St. Elmo's Fire – April 4th 2013

I've been thinking a lot recently about the ties between drinking and low self-esteem, the inextricable link that connects excessive alcohol consumption (known to depress the central nervous system and cause serious chemical imbalances within the brain, resulting in depression and anxiety) and feelings of low self-worth and reduced confidence.

We live in a world that presents us with a multitude of false ideals and unrealistic goals, prizes that are laid just out of reach but always close enough to keep us desperately working to possess them.

The dangerously unrealistic media ideal of who each of us is, whether a teenager, a mum, a grandparent, a husband, a wife, a man, or a woman, is plastered onto the adverts, films and TV programmes, magazines and newspapers which circulate our daily lives and infiltrate our comprehension of 'normal' at every turn. It can be an inordinately difficult task to reject such societal norms and rest comfortably in our own skin, safe in the knowledge that we do our best each day and are happy with our lot − modest though it may be.

For someone who has the added vulnerability of poor self-esteem, for those who spend their days struggling to feel up to scratch, unworthy of anybody else's respect and simply unable to measure up to what they believe is expected of them, this unattainable illusion of perfection serves to grind them down, deeper and deeper into the mire of insignificance.

Alcohol provides an obvious respite from such self-loathing − its immediate (albeit temporary) effect of false confidence and its canny function of ameliorating the day's worries and concerns make it an easy remedy for the pain of feeling not good enough. Knowing that alcohol is so readily available adds to its perennial charm, it's inviting and reassuring calling from the shop up the road all too easy to hear as the day draws to a close.

The trouble is, as I discovered to my detriment, alcohol undergoes very quickly a character transformation of its own when you drink too much of it; from confidence-booster to kicking you while you are down, shoulder to cry on to slap around the face. The things you do when you're under the influence and the things that you don't do when you are under the influence very slowly build up and induce feelings of self-hatred. Too much alcohol makes lazy underachievers out of us, preventing us from pursuing anything worthwhile, as we are more often than not drunk or hungover. And the unattainable versions of whom we think we should be, the pictures in the magazines and the people on the big screen, they become further and further away from who we are, rendering us lost, drowning in a sticky mess of negativity and hopelessness.

And when self-confidence is then so reduced, it becomes increasingly difficult to hold on to any sense of what's real and what's not; the line between truth and make-believe is blurred and, without ever really noticing, we slide into a dangerous game of drawing unfavourable comparisons between who we think we are and what 'everyone else' is. Except they aren't that, they aren't what we think they are – they are just not suffering from chronically low self-esteem and terrible anxiety attacks. The short bursts of false confidence that arise after a drink provide confusing snapshots of who we think we are; the fun-loving party animal, the vivacious, flirtatious sex bomb, the deep and interesting conversationalist who holds everyone in raptures as she talks confidently about all sorts … where is she in the morning?

She is nowhere to be found – as real as a ghost, a puff of smoke escaping through an open window.

With a clear head and a healthy, balanced mind, the differences between alcohol-befuddlement and a normally functioning brain are sharp and vast – the world is suddenly viewed through a sparklingly clean window, rather than a tainted lens coloured by smears of dirt. Without alcohol, the world is still a place in which we can sometimes be made to feel slightly below par, but it is one in which we have a fighting chance of retaining our sense of self, of forging emotional wellbeing and personal growth. When we are no longer poisoning our minds, we allow ourselves to be who we are meant to be – we cease to fight against nature.

Two Years to Self-Esteem – April 9th 2013

I stopped drinking two years ago. I have learnt a lot in those twenty-four months about how the body and mind repair themselves after years of being subjected to alcohol abuse, and seen how it is possible to leave behind a very negative persona, full of self-doubt, low confidence, and insecurities, and replace her with someone who lives and breathes optimism, self-confidence, and contentment.

One of the most difficult obstacles to overcome when attempting to adopt a sober lifestyle is that, when first embarking on this new pathway, the newly teetotal person has very low feelings of self-worth, and the powerful and persuasive inner voice that screams out 'you don't deserve anything good in life anyway so why try to be happy?' is difficult to ignore.

When I first emerged from that nightmarish tunnel of relentless drinking and all the awful associations that go with it, I hated myself. I found it very hard to hold a conversation with someone and hold their eye contact. I did not believe in my abilities at all, I felt as though I were inferior to everyone. I had no real ambitions because I could not conceive of ever achieving anything worthwhile; I would've struggled to come up with a list of ten things I liked about me.

When you have such a low opinion of yourself, it is a constant battle to stay away from alcohol, because it is all too easy to fall into the trap of believing that you don't deserve a better life than the one from which you are trying to escape.

Over time – and this is why I am writing this today, for anyone who is fighting the urge to give in to alcohol and all its temptations in the early days of sobriety – your belief in yourself grows. Gradually you begin to think of yourself as a decent human being who is worth more than simply accepting their lot as a muted, sloshed, semiconscious, unhealthy, foolish, out-of-control, full-of-shame drunk, and you do consider other possibilities. Alternative lifestyle choices begin to spring up around you and, surprisingly at first, you take them.

After a sufficient amount of time has passed, it becomes an incongruous idea that you might pick up a glass of toxic liquid and drink it with the full knowledge that it will transform you into a different person. Your heart will beat faster, your words will begin to slur, you will spout nonsense, you'll lose your sense of who you are, you will embarrass yourself by saying or doing something silly, you'll wake up feeling dehydrated and ill, you will berate yourself for how you acted, you'll snap at your kids, your performance at work will be below par, you won't like yourself, you will look awful.

And with time comes such self-awareness and a feeling of actually liking yourself, that presented with the chance of having an alcoholic drink, you genuinely come to think 'Urrgh, why would I ever do that to myself?'

At least, that's how it has turned out for me.

Life Goes on – April 11th 2013

There was a time when I would never have believed I'd be sitting here writing about how I beat alcohol addiction in my mid-thirties. Wine was such an integral part of my life that imagining my existence without it there on the kitchen side, cork removed, silently breathing, the reassuring tinkling of liquid as it flowed into a large wine glass, hazy nights and regretful mornings never complete without the obligatory pounding head and collection of empties to clear up off the coffee table would have been akin to considering spending a day without air.

I'm used to not drinking now. I know the feelings of sadness and hurt – I know when I'm angry and happy and bored and frustrated. I understand myself and have felt each and every emotion as it seeps through my entire being and just is – no anaesthetic and no disguises.

Occasionally I feel as though I might burst, the intensity of raw sentiment wells up and the knowledge that I can't get rid of it, treat it with something, force it out of myself is overwhelming. It takes practice to learn how to deal with those moments.

Every once in a while there's a blow to the heart that hurts so much it feels like a thousand little punches to the chest. If you resist a drink, the pain won't instantly disappear – sobriety is not the giver of eternal happiness, silently moving in to mop up the tears and wrap you in comfort. Feeling your emotions, without using alcohol to wash them away like driftwood lost to the tide, means knowing highs and lows. The lows remind me of grieving elephants, engulfed by their sadness; the highs are paradise on earth, taking me by joyful surprise whenever one comes along.

Being sober means living through emotions, and finding the strength and dignity to cope with the rough and the smooth. It takes time to get it right but it is, in my opinion, well worth the fight. Once in a while I feel so much pain that it catches my breath and I think I might be choking on air. But it passes soon enough, logic and resilience return, and I move on. And the next day brings a fresh start – which will for ever be preferable to waking up to the legacy of the previous night's alcohol frenzy.

'Life goes on' actually means something when you're sober. It's a truism.

Joie de Vivre – April 13th 2013

Some people can drink alcohol moderately and manage to maintain a happy, balanced life.

Some people cannot.

Alcohol can make you feel happy, sexy, confident and full of joie de vivre.

Alcohol can make you feel desperately unhappy, full of self-hatred, anxious and sick.

Drinking is a social event, a 'thing' that seems to be all around us.

Being teetotal can make you feel somewhat left out.

Nobody can make you stop drinking, so if you choose, you can continue to drink until you die.

Nobody can make you continue to drink, so if you choose, you never have to drink alcohol again.

Some people can take or leave alcohol.

Some people can't seem to stop drinking once they begin.

Some people want to reach self-fulfilment.

Alcohol is marketed in a way which can make it appear to be sophisticated and cool.

Alcohol is the root cause of thousands of deaths every year.

Alcohol can negatively skew your vision of your world.

You possess the ability to choose what works best for you in your life.

You are the mistress of your own destiny.

Turning the Other Cheek – April 18th 2013

The devil will, I believe, always be within spitting distance of my mind. I'll have days when I ponder the notion that perhaps now, after all this time, I could have just one little drink. That sneaky voice, pervasive and persuasive, will once in a while pop up and proposition me with the questions of 'did you really need to stop for good?' and 'how about you simply exercise some alcohol moderation?' and 'don't you know that time heals all?' I will still, occasionally, feel a tugging on my collar as the demon attempts to lure me back into his den of destruction.

Why can I now resist what I never could during all those drunken years of my past? My sober persistence stems from learning a lesson, accepting the truth, and keeping myself firmly on a path that leads in the opposite direction. Being sober and true to myself doesn't mean that I no longer hear the call – it simply means that now I understand the need to ignore it, and that over time I have gradually developed the tools to silence it.

Not drinking alcohol for two years does not eradicate the inability to drink 'sensibly.' Avoiding booze for a sufficient length of time does not magically dissolve the desire to consume the whole bottle just as soon as you pop the cork and swallow your first mouthful. But what time without alcohol does provide is enough self-awareness to allow you to recognise your weak spots, your triggers, and your instincts.

Living alcohol-free allows you to develop the knowledge that your brain operates on two levels; this is commonly referred to as being ruled by your head or your heart, or having your angel on one shoulder and the devil on the other. Given enough time without alcohol sullying your ability to think clearly, it becomes second nature to spot which is the 'bad brain' talking and which is you.

A little like being a child and having a naughty friend who coerces you into causing trouble with them, and a good, loyal friend who respects you and values your feelings above his or her own, understanding which of your two brains to listen to means arriving at the realisation of what's right for you, and what works best in your happy life.

So when you hear that little voice whispering sweet nothings in your ear and attempting to draw you back to where you ran so desperately from once upon a time, try and regard it as the bad friend – turn the other cheek and seek out what's right. *You* will thank you for your strength in the morning.

We're Going to the Zoo – April 22nd 2013

Yesterday I visited London Zoo with my two daughters, my fiancé, and his sister. We sauntered about in the sunshine, taking in the tigers, lions, penguins, monkeys, and other animals before catching the tube back to my almost-sister-in-law's house amongst tired marathon runners wrapped in aluminium foil.

I was reminded that having a day out is a fantastic way to remove yourself from the stresses that we all feel subjected to in our daily lives to some degree, the perfect way to avoid over-thinking a problem or flinging yourself between a multitude of household chores, weighted down with an inability to relax.

As a drinker, I could not relax unless I had a glass of wine in my hand (and the knowledge that a fairly substantial supply was present somewhere in my vicinity). I would hurtle between jobs at a hundred miles an hour before finally, at a designated and preconceived time, plonking down on the settee with a large glass of vino that said obnoxiously to anyone else present, "OK, this is my time – you can ask but my responses will be limited from this point onwards."

As a non-drinker, I have discovered other ways of relaxing which are far more effective than alcohol ever was. Nowadays when I switch off, I am still present and able to respond to people if they really need me, and most definitely remain in control of my faculties; this self-awareness means that I always listen to my body and act accordingly – drinking excessively always perked me up and ostensibly eradicated all notions of tiredness, making me believe that I was full of beans and that it would be a great idea to stay up until 3 a.m. on a school night watching mindless drivel on the TV or listening to my back catalogue of 'songs from the good old days'. In reality I was exhausted and alcohol only served to make me more so.

Having a day out at the zoo not only helped me to unwind during the time I spent there, it has had a lasting effect on my state of mind as I am reminded of the importance of spending quality time with my family, having some fun, and living in the present whenever possible.

We spent a while at the giraffe enclosure, observing those beautiful creatures eating the carrots offered to them by some other visitors to the zoo. Their lofty amble across the paddock as they wandered towards the food held out on offer to them was a lesson in insouciant deportment – it was difficult to imagine them ever feeling stressed out over anything.

Conversely, human beings can be terrific stress bombs, overwrought with anxieties and fears, largely concerning things that most likely will never happen and even if they do, will not be as terrible as previously imagined. It is a worthwhile day out that reminds us of the fact that yesterday has gone and tomorrow is not certain, and that therefore the only time we really have is today.

I like to think that giraffes work on this basis.

Lifesaver – April 26th 2013

The sun comes up, the traffic begins to build as workers set out for the day, and I put on my trainers and lead the dog out on to the pavement for our morning run. It's just another day. There is a chill in the air but the icy breath of winter has been superseded by a more tolerable spring breeze. Buses roll past me, undertaking the static cars powerless to move faster in the morning rush-hour jam. It's just another day.

Back at the house I check my phone and notice the date, 26th April. It's a friend's birthday.

He's much more than a friend actually. He's my lifesaver.

Approximately 725 days ago the friend whose birthday it is found me unconscious in the dark, alone and drunk and vomiting. He called an ambulance, rode in it with me, sat by my bedside for hours in the stark glare of the hospital ward, told me it was OK when I woke up, looked at me with sadness, held my hand, helped me discharge myself, and took me home in a taxi. He put me to bed, made me a cup of tea, told me it would be OK, told me *I* would be OK, and didn't leave until I had stopped crying.

I never really thought I had been within touching distance of my own death until that morning. The weeks that followed were the darkest I've ever known. But eventually the sun came out again, and I moved forward.

The friend who saved my life gave me so much to be grateful for; the chance to live free of the shackles of alcohol, room to grow as a person, all the days I've spent since with my two children, fiancé, and my family, a deep appreciation of everything I have in my life, my health and happiness, a real awareness of the fragility of life and, with that, a passion for so much that the world has to offer, developing a realisation of the things that matter, and the things that don't, my future hopes and dreams, becoming who I was meant to be, my life.

I sent him a text. It read 'Happy birthday Lifesaver. Lots of love, always.' And I meant it.

Believe in the Power of Fear – April 28th 2013

I am a big believer in doing what you are scared of. As I watch my twelve-month-old crawl around the house with absolutely no sense of fear, it strikes me as obvious that this is how human beings grow and develop awareness of their surroundings. Because she isn't scared of attempting the monumental flight of stairs that rise up before her, or to make the descent off the end of the bed head first, Lily gets on with things and learns valuable lessons, such as balance, concentration, focus, and so on. If she were paralysed by fear she would never attempt anything new and would stagnate at the toddler stage of development for ever.

As we mature, life delivers a series of (often harsh) lessons that alter the course of our behaviour. We experience something horrible, a memory is created, and the next time something similar arises we are naturally cautious. This, together with an increasing sense of mortality, can bring us to a point where we fail to try anything new or remotely scary.

Over the last few years, the events that have frightened me the most are as follows: childbirth, skydiving, flying (particularly taking off and landing), and stopping drinking.

I think you can see where I am going with this – every one of these situations ultimately brought me nothing but immense joy and satisfaction, together with a huge step forward in my personal development. I have only ever known true fear when facing what turned out to be the highlights of my life.

As both my pregnancies approached their natural conclusions I was overwhelmed with a morbid sense of terror regarding the perceived pain and potential medical complications. As the tiny Cessna aircraft climbed to the 10,000 feet drop point, I thought I would literally die with fright – I was utterly petrified and the only reason I actually managed to make the jump was because I was strapped to a man who was clearly going to ignore any protestations on my part about falling two miles to the ground in a matter of minutes.

The biggie for me was facing my fear of sobriety. For reasons which now appear ridiculous, I was scared to death about living my life free from the grip of addiction; terrified of living with clarity and self-awareness, unsure of the person I would be without the stupidity and boring behaviour brought about by my reckless binge-drinking. I had a deep sense of foreboding that my life was on the brink of collapse, and that I was facing the rest of my days bored and ascetic, a shadow of my former self.

Fear is there to be faced and overcome. Nowadays, whenever something frightens me and my stomach becomes filled with that familiar knot, I remind myself that only good things have ever been born from my fears. I dig deep for courage and just do it.

Take Good Care of Your Self-Esteem – April 30th 2013

What happens to so many people in our society as they grow from children to adults and in the process gradually shed their self-belief and confidence? From my mid-teens until the age of thirty-five I was caught up in an alcohol dependency that became so deeply embedded in who I thought I was that the revelation of the real me which came to light after becoming teetotal came as a huge surprise.

As a child I was brimming with self-confidence, a little bit stubborn, a high achiever and natural leader. I threw myself gung-ho into whatever activity I was doing and thought I would reach nothing less than amazing and dizzy heights of success in whatever field I chose to venture into – post Oxbridge, of course.

Oh, how reality bites – by age fourteen I was drinking regularly, smoking, obsessed with boys, rather less obsessed with school work, and venturing ever nearer to the brink of an eating disorder which fully took hold a few months later. Over the course of the next five years, my self-belief nosedived and by the time I was 20 I was living with an ex-con, drinking like a fish, and struggling to get through my degree course. I hardly ate, smoked twenty a day, and had no desire to do anything with my time other than get absolutely out of my head.

I don't really have any definitive answers for the puzzle of how that happened. I came from a happy and secure family, I wasn't bullied at school, and there were no major traumas from which I bore deep mental scars. The only constants in the trajectory of my youth, twenties, and early thirties were alcohol and cigarettes.

As I spend my life now without the crutch of alcohol, or of any other addiction (excluding coffee and chocolate, but they constitute small-fry in comparison to previous vices), it seems entirely probable that the somewhat skewed path that my life took prior to quitting alcohol two years ago was as a direct result of too much booze. I was permanently depressed as a consequence of all that wine, I neglected to eat properly owing to a huge lack of self-esteem and some misguided belief that if I was super thin I would be super happy, and not eating caused me to suffer terrible mood swings; I self-medicated these with more wine, and the alcohol was also responsible for many of the poor choices of partner that I made over the years – many of whom I would never have been within 10 yards of had I been sober.

I see my fourteen-year-old daughter now caught like a rabbit in the headlights, choosing whether to believe in something good for herself, or throwing it all to one side and getting on with the business of self-contempt. It seems that, especially for women, developing a sense of low self-worth is perceived as interesting at best, romantic at worse. As a teenager I fell for it hook, line, and sinker, filling my head with sexy notions of messed-up women, the idea that falling into a state of vulnerability and despair would somehow enhance my attractiveness; a Betty Blue for Sheffield.

Today, as a strong, positive, and determined woman of thirty-seven, I see nothing to shy away from in the idea of a woman being together and able to take care of herself and her family without the need for a crutch of any sort (apart from the chocolate and the coffee – see above).

It is now my mission to pass this ideal on to my wonderful, intelligent, capable, and strong teenage daughter.

One-Way Ticket to Happiness – May 2ⁿᵈ 2013

A few years ago, amidst a period of very heavy drinking, I went on holiday with my then partner and our three children (two of his, one of mine).

Right up until the day we left I had been downing at least a bottle of wine a night, every night, for weeks on end and as a result had experienced a number of distressing events, arguments, traumas, and other assorted booze-related catastrophes.

I made the decision to have an alcohol-free holiday because we were taking our three children with us and I couldn't trust myself to not do or say something terrible that would ruin everyone's memories of that week for ever more.

It was a simple decision to make and a relatively easy one to stick to. We drove down to Cornwall and stayed in a beautiful big house set in rolling green hills and farmland. The sun shone all week and we spent seven days surfing, swimming, eating ice creams, and in the evenings played trivial pursuits and watched films. We caught some amazing waves and I remember one in particular that my ex-partner's daughter, my daughter, and I rode together, the three of us careering towards the beach screaming and laughing at the breathtaking way we had been possessed by the sea.

I spent the week relaxed, happy, and content, relieved not to be waking up each morning with that familiar sense of dread and having to apologise to those around me for my lack of control and inability to realise that I had reached my wine limit but still continued to drink, yet again. How do you apologise to children for being drunk and stupid? You can't really – they don't, and neither should we expect them to, understand.

However, as was my way back then, I reached the end of the holiday feeling refreshed and full of vigour, tanned, happy, and free, and then hit the bottle again upon reaching home. It would take me a further five years to stop for good.

As we approach this year's holiday to Cornwall in a few weeks' time I am not in a position where I need to consider whether to cut out alcohol or not for the seven days I spend with my fiancé and two daughters in a caravan near the sea. I am lucky enough to have reached a stage in my life where I know I will never put myself through the torment of substance abuse ever again. My holiday at the end of May will be the same as every other holiday I will take during the rest of my life – a relaxing break which doesn't involve booze, regrets, and hangovers.

Drinking on holiday for me was like going sailing in a

boat with a hole in the bottom – it starts out being fun but soon enough it's going to sink and take everyone down with it.

Sticks and Stones – May 7th 2013

Labelling human beings is not good. Once you have been pigeon-holed by society it is extraordinarily difficult to rid yourself of that tag and carve out a new definition of who you are.

In the early weeks of my new teetotal life I came to the conclusion that I was 'an alcoholic'. I remember clear as day admitting this terrible truth to myself, something I had been shying away from for years, and finally, crushingly, wearily nodding in quiet acceptance of the fact that I was diseased and would for ever be a troubled soul who needed to rebuff all temptation of drinking alcohol in order to avoid the dreaded relapse.

My self-esteem was at an all-time low back then. Labelling myself 'an alcoholic' only added fuel to the fire as the word evoked feelings of failure and weakness. I was consumed with a sense of powerlessness but plodded on regardless with my desire to live in sobriety, hoping that eventually I would feel something more than abject misery.

As the weeks turned into months I changed my perspective and I now look back on my drinking years as a couple of decades in which I drank way too much and was most definitely dependent (emotionally and mentally) upon, and probably rather in love with, alcohol. When I stopped drinking I experienced no physical withdrawal symptoms, merely a tough internal battle to rid myself of the mental cravings and urges that I had given in to for so many years and were therefore pretty difficult to overcome.

For a fairly long period, maybe a year, I also had to

discover who I really was beneath the booze, learn to deal with my emotions like a grown-up instead of pouring anaesthetic liquid down my neck at the slightest sign of trouble, overcome a multitude of regrets, and develop interests in activities other than boozing in order to fill my time.

In weaving my way through the jungle of emotional baggage I'd acquired as someone who drinks too much, I slowly became a non-addicted human being, free of dependencies on any mind-altering substances, just a regular person who sees life through the untainted lens of sober vision. I dropped the notion that I was and always would be 'an alcoholic,' as the idea that you are suffering from an addiction when you haven't touched the substance in question for two years and have absolutely no desire to ever do so again just seems plain weird.

I am in no doubt that if I had a drink then I would be back where I started from pretty quickly, but in the same way that someone with a nut allergy would avoid nuts like the plague but never label themselves a 'nut addict' for doing so, I cannot conceive of being an 'alcoholic' purely on the basis that I know now that alcohol and I do not, and will never, complement one another.

If you have recently begun living (or are considering doing so) a healthy alcohol-free life then I would avoid labelling yourself 'an alcoholic'. It is a damaging term that is rife with negative connotations and which often sparks off prejudices that are difficult to fight, particularly when you are already at a low ebb. Referring to yourself in that way can also help consolidate the idea that you are powerless in the face of a disease, when in reality you are master or mistress of your own destiny – *you* can decide to stop drinking, and in doing so you will learn to overcome the mental or emotional dependency that you have on alcohol.

In the end, 'alcoholic' is just a word, so ask yourself the

question of what's more important; an arbitrary collection of letters, or having the best possible chance at living happily and free of a dependency on anything but yourself?

Proud – May 8th 2013

I only have three pieces of jewellery that I have a sentimental attachment to; my engagement ring, a silver bracelet that my elder daughter bought me last Christmas, and the orange disc bracelet that I ordered to commemorate my commitment to life as a Soberista and which arrived this morning.

I had the date of the Soberistas website launch engraved on it, 26.11.12 and the word 'Soberistas' and I am wearing it with pride! When I look at the bracelet it makes me remember all the fantastic things in my life that have happened as a result of stopping drinking, of all the amazing people who help each other every day on Soberistas, how my life really began properly when I decided to live it alcohol-free and how I will never let myself get as low as I was just two years ago, ever again.

I can't take the credit for the idea of wearing a Soberistas bracelet – Katey and Josephinerina are the ones to thank for that! But I am so grateful to them for thinking up such a positive and proud way to celebrate their new lives as Soberistas. I absolutely love wearing my little orange tribute to my sobriety!

Oh, I Don't Drink! – May 10th 2013

I had a funny moment today when a sudden, out-of-the-blue thought sprang up and disrupted my quiet, plodding along, morning brain. I don't know what prompted it but landing squarely and suddenly at the forefront of my mind were these words; 'I don't drink, I am a non-drinker, I have become somebody who does not ever touch alcohol … as if I have certain religious beliefs that forbid me from drinking alcohol, I just never, ever drink.'

This internal confirmation of my teetotal commitment tumbled rudely into my chain of thoughts and made me catch my breath. If you had known me before I stopped drinking you would know why. I never, ever imagined that I would be a person who did not drink booze. I used to be, very simply, a drinker – it's what I was known for.

I recall going for dinner at a boyfriend's parents' house in my late teens, his father being a wine connoisseur who enjoyed indulging in his love of fine wines in the company of guests. Upon settling into the sumptuous settee before we ate I was handed a glass of something red and fantastically expensive. As he passed me the elegant wine glass, the father's eyes bored into mine and he said sternly, 'This is a *very* good wine – please do not guzzle it.' He totally had my number.

When I look back over photographs stretching back twenty years I see alcohol featuring in almost all of them; holiday snaps, Christmases, birthdays, nights out, nights in – life was one very long and raucous party and I was usually to be found slap bang in the middle of it, shining in the spotlight, always drinking.

I have worked very hard on being sober and happy over the last couple of years; it didn't come easy and I have expended a lot of time and energy in my acceptance of this radical departure from old destructive habits. I think I've been so busy with ensuring I am OK about not drinking that the end result has almost arrived unnoticed – that is to say the transition from colossal pisshead to totally straight person has happened amidst such a sea of change that this morning's sudden and stark thought surprised me.

Me? Teetotal? Now there's something I thought I would never say. I am now so definitively a non-drinker whereas once I was defined by my enormous affection for wine and enthusiasm for losing myself in the maddening, mind-altering, crazed mayhem that it initiated in me. Five years ago I would have bet large amounts of money on me drinking my way through life until the alcoholic sun eventually sank on my world and plunged everything in it into complete blackness.

Today I am better – very different, but very much better – which is kind of surprising.

Finding Your Way Out of the Darkness – May 14th 2013

During my alcohol-fuelled past life I was so ashamed of my little boozy secret, particularly the lonely drinking and the inability to stop once I'd begun, that I covered up the negativity with a hefty dose of bravado and a tenacious refusal to let my hangovers get in the way of life.

Behind the runs I would force myself to go on the morning after a binge, beneath the smiles at work and the heavy make-up to conceal the facial signs of my hangovers, I was completely beset with agonising emotional pain and heartache caused by what I perceived as my failure to 'drink like normal people do'.

I couldn't admit to myself that I had a problem so I was never going to offload my awful secret to anyone else. And so I continued to drink to help forget about the inner turmoil, and I refused to fully acknowledge what I now recognise as a serious dependency upon alcohol.

At my lowest ebb I could barely look another human being in the eye. I stopped caring about the level of harm I was inflicting on my physical self, and conversely I harboured thoughts pertaining to hurting myself and the pointlessness of my life.

For a long time since becoming free of alcohol I haven't experienced any real depression or sadness as my life has tended to go from strength to strength ever since I put down the bottle. But I clearly remember the weighty burden of depression and how it made making even the simplest of decisions a frightening and exhausting task of epic proportions.

This is why it can be so incredibly hard to make the choice to stop drinking – the short-term relief from the feelings of sadness and depression that can be found in alcohol is so tempting in its false ameliorative quality that to find the strength to rebuff it in your darkest of hours is challenging, to say the least. And even if you are aware of the negative repercussions of drinking alcohol, when depressed and consumed by self-loathing it is often the intention to inflict further misery on yourself, as opposed to seeking a way out of your depression and into happiness once again.

The thing with all of the above is that if you can find the motivation to stop drinking while feeling so low, fairly soon you will notice a lift in your mood and will gradually witness the rejuvenation of your self-esteem. And when this happens, you will no longer have the intense desire to hurt yourself, rather the opposite will be true; you will want to look after yourself and live a happy existence. In not much time at all, the negative blinkers will fall by the wayside and the world will open up to you as a place filled with possibilities and potential – the restrictive, bleak future that you had mapped out for yourself fading into nothingness.

It is a hugely difficult and brave thing to take the first step into a new life which you cannot see or even imagine, but it is only the first few footsteps which you will have to navigate in the darkness; once you have made it so far, the sun will come out and shine up a path right before your eyes – a path which you will truly want to follow.

As Martin Luther King, Jr. once said, "Faith is taking the first step even when you don't see the whole staircase."

Freedom to Fly – May 18th 2013

For me, regularly drinking alcohol generated terrible feelings of being worthless and inferior to everyone else I ever came into contact with. In addition, this destructive assault on my self-belief always came to the fore simultaneously with a hefty dose of what can only be described as 'negative mental attitude'.

It was the world's fault that I did not achieve what I wanted in life, that my marriage had ended in its infancy, that I hated my job, that I was struggling financially – there was always someone else to blame – never me.

One of the greatest gifts of sobriety is the joyful return to living in the real world. Occasionally there are difficult patches which must be navigated through, and not drinking certainly does not make life a guaranteed bed of roses. What living alcohol-free does provide, however, is a reality check and a realisation that while things may not always be quite how you would choose, you are equipped with all the tools required to make the best of your hand.

Instead of enduring a crippling dose of internal criticism whenever I meet a person whom I deem to be superior in some respect to me, I now recognise their plus points as nice qualities which I admire, rather than an emotional hand grenade to hurl at my fragile sense of self; so if someone is very pretty I consider her as, well, being pretty; as in: 'She's pretty – wow, what gorgeous hair/eyes/cheekbones'. This is infinitely healthier than the old alternative of 'Oh my God, she is so beautiful. Look at me in comparison; I am fat, ugly, with horrible hair, awful clothes, and generally hideous. I must run home at once and hide away until I forget that I ever had the misfortune to stand near this stunning creature.'

Nowadays I recognise that while I have my plus points and am neither hideously ugly nor out-of-this-world beautiful, I am just fine the way I am. If I meet people who are prettier/cleverer/wittier/more interesting than I am then it's a pleasure being in their company and enjoying their special qualities. I have come to understand that there will always be someone who is doing something or looking better than I will ever be able to, and people who have amazing physiques that I will probably never attain, and people who are fortunate enough to have long, flowing, glossy tresses which I know I will never be able to grow.

But that's OK, because they will never have what I have either.

Not drinking stops the endless cycle of self-loathing and negativity caused by depression and alcohol-induced shame. Living alcohol-free allows you to come forth like a butterfly emerging from a cocoon and to subsequently realise all your qualities that have previously been smothered by alcohol for so long.

Give yourself a chance; stop drinking and spread your wings.

Goodnight – May 21st 2013

I've noticed over the last few months how much I love my bedtime. I do have an extremely busy life and am usually exhausted by the time I make my way upstairs to bed, and this could be a contributing factor, but since living alcohol-free I have developed a real fondness for hitting the hay.

Night time used to mean drinking; whether at home or out with friends, when the sun went down the wine came out and bedtime was consequently a drunken affair that I barely remembered in the morning (or I would collapse on the settee where I remained comatose and fully clothed until dawn).

At the risk of sounding a little like an old lady, I now find myself enjoying the entire routine of taking my make-up off, putting comfortable pyjamas on, and snuggling under the duvet with the low-level spotlights creating just enough light for me to read by. When the lights go out I think of all the things I will be doing the next day and feel a sense of happy anticipation for tomorrow, even when there is nothing in particular to be looking forward to. I mentally run over the day I have just had and think of the especially good moments, or reflect on the things which perhaps didn't go as I had hoped.

This is most likely a totally normal experience for many people but I'm still enjoying the novelty of it – not waking up with a horrible dry mouth at 5 a.m., no awful arguments or regrettable incidents to agonise over in the dark, early hours when the only company you have is the deeply painful self-hatred that fills every fibre of your being.

I love my cleansers and night moisturisers, my new pyjamas from M&S, the pile of books by my bedside, the feeling of health and freedom of mind, and the knowledge that there will be nothing to be sorry for in the morning. I love feeling sleepy, and that the physical and mental tiredness is due to the fact that I have worked hard all day and pushed myself to be the best I can be. I love knowing that I won't look like hell in the morning, even if I'm up during the night with the baby. I love thinking of all the lovely people I have in my life.

I love living and sleeping alcohol-free.

Read this and then Forget the Word 'Failure' – May 23rd 2013

Forget the word failure. Calling yourself a failure is akin to puncturing your lifeboat as you escape a sinking ship – alcohol has damaged your self-esteem. In order to break free from the booze trap, you need as much self-esteem as you can get your hands on; labelling yourself anything negative at this juncture serves absolutely no purpose. And anyway, you never set out to get into this mess. Alcohol is an addictive and widely/cleverly marketed substance and you are only human. Give yourself a break and drop the 'failure' tag.

Allow yourself some time to recover from your dependency on alcohol. This won't happen overnight and can be a long and painful process. Don't give in to temptation simply because you don't feel amazing after three weeks – you should be in this for the long haul. Remember that the reason you are stopping drinking is because you want to feel happy and healthy again; that is worth waiting for.

Independent and strong is how you will feel if you can stay true to your intentions and remain alcohol-free. It is a wonderful and freeing sensation knowing that you are master of your own destiny, rather than being ruled by a bottle of plonk.

Life is precious – you only get one chance at it. The

day will come when you'll look back at all you have achieved (or not) and you won't be able to turn round and do things differently – it's a one-way road. Grab the opportunity to change your destiny with both hands. Make yourself proud of whomever you become, and start the process today.

Underneath all the anxiety and depression that alcohol causes there is a happy, free spirit who enjoys even the simplest things, finding pleasure in everyday life. If you stop drinking, that person will emerge like a butterfly from a cocoon and you'll be amazed that she existed inside without you even realising she was there.

Reap the rewards that an alcohol-free life brings: more energy, levelled-out moods, weight loss, better skin, increased creativity and productivity, more interest in other people, a heightened desire to set and reach goals, restored self-esteem, and the eradication of excessive anxiety and stress can all be yours if you adopt an alcohol-free life.

Enjoy the feeling of being back in control – forget the word failure. Failure is simply a barrier to your happiness, and whoever decided that you did not have the right to be happy? Put 'failure' where it belongs – in the bin along with the booze. *You* deserve better.

Holiday Diary – May 31st 2013

We've been on holiday for three days, making home out of a static caravan nestled in the low-lying hills of Holywell Bay, near Newquay, Cornwall. We are positioned in a spot which is devoid of any possibility of communicating with the outside world, our mobiles displaying absolutely no telephone reception or 3G connection signs. That's OK– I'm taking it as a good thing, an opportunity to lessen my dependence on incoming and outgoing digital messages of all kinds and to concentrate on real life for a few days.

Strangely enough I haven't missed Twitter or Facebook or even text messaging in any way. The absolute removal of its availability has resulted in my resignation to living how we did last time I came to this caravan park eleven years ago, when mobiles hadn't yet taken over our lives, my elder daughter was just three, I was married to her dad, I was a heavy drinker, and life was, in almost every way, completely different.

The caravan park is set at the foot of a long winding road, away from passing traffic. Holywell Bay itself is a short walk across sand dunes and is a calm haven of old-fashioned seaside postcard imagery: boogie boarders and surfers, toddlers and windshields, coffee and ice-cream huts, Atlantic rollers and small pools, enormous hulks of rock jutting from the waves, and miles and miles of deep blue-green ocean stretching back to the sky.

On our first day at the beach the sun is out and the wind cuts a fresh breeze, casting a healthy-looking tan on our faces. The baby is in her element, on hands and knees and overwhelmed with the vast expanse of trillions of 'bits' as far as her eyes can see. She grabs handfuls of sand and small shrapnel of seashells and attempts to wolf them down, only to be intercepted by our hands pulling her fist away from her open mouth over and over again. We sit and watch the world go by and take photographs of the baby in her sunhat and flowery playsuit.

There is simplicity in living in a caravan with no internet connection. I find myself contemplating situations and mulling over the factors of my life back home – my relationships and friendships, my weaknesses and strengths. I am spending hours doing nothing in particular; a drive to Fistral Beach, sitting next to the baby in her pram, watching as she gazes curiously at the seagulls whirling in the sky above us, flicking through magazines, perusing the bikinis and hairstyles worn by models and film stars with my teenage daughter, assessing the selection of leaflets left out on the coffee table in order to plan our activities for the next few days, nipping out for an ice cream, taking the baby for a play on the swings and slides in the caravan park.

It reminds me of being young – you fill your time with pleasant pastimes and in between the trips out there is a sense of relaxation, contentment, and none of the hectic pinballing from chore to chore, appointment to appointment, work piling up around your ears and demands placed on you relentlessly, all of which define your existence at home.

It is as though the channels that deliver all the busyness into my life have been barricaded, preventing any of the usual grating stress factors from reaching me and creating a quiet blue space of calm. And I'm just floating here in a different existence where all that matters is the present. Days have become long once again; time has stopped pouring so rapidly through the egg timer, falling through the slim glass neck with increasing speed, slipping out of my grasp.

This afternoon we are visiting the Eden Project. Last time I was there it was newly opened, full to bursting with hordes of interested visitors and I had the hangover from hell which ruined the experience completely. Today's visit to the alien white biomes at St Austell will, I hope, be somewhat more enjoyable.

Re-writing the Past – June 2nd 2013

Lying in bed earlier this morning and feeling somewhat grotty (I seem to have picked up OH's bug), an image of me aged about nineteen popped into my head and triggered a whole range of emotions. This vision of me that appeared from out of nowhere was slim and carefree, dressed in a monochrome outfit, my hair in a bob and on my way to some do or other. I remember what I was wearing clearly – everything from my white Morgan handbag, of which I was extremely proud, down to the black pumps – but it was my mood that I recalled most strongly this morning and which caused me to react with sadness at how the years seem to have taken something away from me.

On that day I was with my ex-boyfriend and despite being held fast in the clutches of an eating disorder and simultaneously abusing alcohol during that phase of my life (not a fantastic combination; drinking a bottle or two of red when you haven't eaten for a few days is an excellent way to pass out very quickly, if that's what floats your boat) I do remember possessing a light sense of freedom from responsibilities, of not knowing enough about the world to have any real worries about the future, and having a lack of awareness of the true implications of my frequently self-centred actions which in actuality hurt people far more than I ever knew back then. The world appeared open to me, full of possibility.

I suppose I was living in a bubble, protecting myself from reality by obsessing over food and living for my social life, frequently drinking myself into oblivion at wild parties and exciting trips away, and never staying sober long enough to think about the things that mattered. This morning, though, I momentarily wished for that sense of freedom back again, the feeling of having nothing to worry about other than how to fill the day ahead – a sense of being young.

I saw a therapist a few years ago who told me I had been emotionally frozen in my teens as a result of my various addictions. I think he was spot on. In the last couple of years since stopping drinking I've grown up fast and it's been a bumpy ride; I've raced through years of emotional maturation in a very short space of time and now it's as though things are finally slowing down and I've been able to look around and see where I'm at for the first time in years.

That image of me in the black-and-white dress is an illusion; the floating cloud I lived on back then was nothing but a figment of my imagination and was therefore unsustainable as a way of spending the rest of my life. The real world is much more, well, real. There was no sense of freedom for me back in the mid-1990s, weighed down as I was by zero self-esteem and addictions that had grown up around me as a way of coping with a deeply engrained self-hatred.

I'm tired (up in the night with baby again), feel ill, and therefore, for just a moment, I fell into harping back to days gone by and seeing only the good – it's the rose-tinted glasses phenomenon, the nostalgia trip that rewrites our pasts, blotting out the bad bits. Twenty years from now I will more than likely look back on my life as it is currently and eliminate the sleepless nights, the not-enough-hours-in-the-day feeling I have during large chunks of my existence and will remember instead only sunny skies, wonderful times with my family, and how grateful I was to be finally out of the drinking trap.

Which are really the only bits that matter.

Flicking the Switch – June 12th 2013

What does it take to flick the switch of alcohol dependency, to really grasp the idea of sobriety by beginning to live a life in which reliance on a mind-altering substance is no longer an integral part?

For twenty years I did not want to stop drinking. For approximately fifteen years of those two decades I was utterly in denial with regards to whether I had 'a drink problem' or not, and happily quaffed bottle upon bottle of white wine, red wine, beer, and spirits (when everything else in the house ran dry), the notion that I was nurturing my addiction each time I popped a cork light years from my mind.

Drinking was never about such a dirty word as 'addiction' – it was sociable, convivial, glamorous, relaxing, a treat, an emotional painkiller, my friend, a closely guarded secret, and a reward for every individual event and activity that I decided warranted further consumption.

But, over time, wine ceased to be my friend – gone were the evenings filled with carefree laughter and tipsiness; silly and relaxed gradually came to be replaced by crazy and comatose. The good times stopped rolling, and when mornings perpetually consist of panicked attempts to piece together the night before coupled with apologising with fake breeziness to those who you have pissed off/hurt/embarrassed yet again while inside you are wincing with the shame of it all, you know that something has got to give.

The switch got flicked. Alcohol was no longer an option – the fanciful nature of it, bottles glistening with beads of condensation in the fridge door, popping corks, big old red wine glasses in which the blood-coloured liquid is swilled round and round releasing its perfume to the nostrils, the reassuring snap of the beer-bottle top being cracked off with the stylish opener, the empties lined up by the back door, the sign of a good night; it all came to an abrupt halt. I knew, finally, that I would never touch the stuff again.

As anyone who has known me for longer than the two years in which I have been alcohol-free would confirm, this shift is nothing short of miraculous. I just didn't want to stop drinking prior to April 2011 – I had my moments of doubt, of wishing things would be different, that I could make something of myself, get on track, push things forward so that my life became full of movement rather than the static black hole I had fallen into – treading water, sinking in quicksand. But I had no real comprehension that the secret to initiating these longed-for changes in my world was to be found in eliminating alcohol. For many years I maintained the position of the switch.

And then, bam! Enough is enough, can't take any more, cannot stand one more awful morning feeling like this, absolutely finished with the awful existence of an addict, done with it, goodbye booze.

And that was it; I just knew I would never drink alcohol again.

A Day not to Forget – June 18th 2013

I had a brilliant day today. Nothing out of the ordinary was planned which may have marked it out as stand-alone from any other Tuesday, although I did wake up feeling full of energy and desperate to go running, and that usually results in a positive start to the day ahead. The sun was beaming and even at 7 a.m. the promise of the glorious day to come was obvious as I jogged around the park, dragging the dog along behind me (she is seven this year and not quite as fit as she once was).

After lunch, baby rejuvenated from her morning sleep of three hours, we did a few jobs around the house before settling into the lounge to play. At fourteen months, Lily has just discovered the incredible concept of putting something inside a container before removing it again, a look of total concentration on her angelic face as if she has happened upon a remarkable piece of magic.

For an hour I lay on the rug next to her as she placed her items into the pots I had lined up. I couldn't take my eyes off her; for sixty minutes we were there – Lily and her very serious face as she put something in, took something out, and me, gazing at her in awe as though she were the first baby on the planet to engage in this activity.

I thought afterwards how grateful I am to the world at large for propelling me along the many different paths in my life which eventually got me to that rug this afternoon with Lily and her selection of pink pots filled with small wooden blocks. Rarely do I manage to fully live in the present and banish all worrisome or niggling thoughts from my mind in order to wholly soak up the here and now, but this afternoon that is precisely what I did and it was magical – I'll remember that passing of time for ever, I just know I will.

Dare to Dream – June 25th 2013

Occasionally I experience the feeling that I am on the outside of my life looking in. Today was one of those days.

This morning with the baby sleeping upstairs, I spent a couple of hours working on the introduction to the book I have been writing (in conjunction with Sarah Turner of the Harrogate Sanctuary) and allowed myself, for the first time, to acknowledge the fact that we are now on the home stretch and therefore have pretty much written an entire book – a real life, full-length book that is one hundred per cent our creation. I couldn't and still can't quite believe it.

I have been banging on to anyone who would listen for years and years that 'I'm writing a book'. There has always been one simmering on the backburner, a few chapters in the bag before I predictably stalled mid-way, never approaching completion – a multitude of never-ending projects for which I couldn't quite muster the energy to make my way to THE END.

I have made it this far with the book we have spent the last few months putting together as a result of sobering up: a) There would be no subject matter if I was still boozing, b) I would never have met Sarah, my brilliant writing partner, had I maintained my alcohol dependency, c) my creativity was completely sapped by alcohol back in the drinking days, and d) I could never have squeezed a project this big and this important into my life amidst all those alcohol-fuelled nights.

So here we are, the last few weeks of work before the writing is finished, the editing done, and the proofreading complete. It feels like such an achievement, not least because this is something which I have been trying to do for almost twenty years. Finally, one of my all-time goals in life has (very nearly) been accomplished.

It just goes to show what you can do when you put down the bottle.

Logic – July 5th 2013

One thing I've got back since I stopped drinking alcohol (apart from a myriad of different elements of the normal human physical and mental condition, which I was never aware were missing when I drank, but now prize so highly) is logical thinking.

In the old days I used to be, on occasion, slightly nuts. I hesitate to spill the beans about this following revelation, as when I recall the night's events I cannot quite believe that I am one and the same person, and it makes me sound somewhat, well, mad.

One Sunday evening, incredibly hungover from the night before and fuzzily drunk after sinking several glasses of hair-of-the-dog wine during the course of the afternoon and early evening, I found myself alone at home and fancying a cigarette. It was autumn and already dark by about 8 p.m. when I stepped on to the threshold of my kitchen door and lit up. At the time, I lived in a tiny terraced house which had no garden, front or back, but a miniscule yard that backed on to a dark alleyway. This concrete space was encased with high brick walls, one of which featured a solid wooden gate which opened into the passage that ran the breadth of the terraced row. The only way into the yard (other than through the gate which was kept locked) was via the kitchen door.

As I stood huddled in pyjamas and woolly cardigan puffing long trails of smoke into the chilly air, my gaze came to rest on a mysterious hump in the corner of the backyard. The low light that seeped out around the kitchen window blinds did not reveal much, but enough to make me arrive at the conclusion that this strange huddle, barely concealed behind a few straggly fronds of ivy, was a capybara.

Yes, you read correctly – I actually imagined that the world's largest rodent, native to South America and relative of the chinchilla and guinea pig, was having a little sit down in the corner of my backyard a few miles out of Sheffield city centre.

Alarmed and (incredibly, I know) frightened, I slowly retreated into the house, closing the door softly so as not to disturb the beast, and called my brave friend in order that he might pop round to sort my little problem out.

When he arrived half an hour later, I hustled him through the house, pushed him urgently through the back door and pointed him in the direction of the capybara. Unsurprisingly, he was laughing quite a lot by this stage, and for want of a better phrase, completely ridiculing me. Torch in hand, he flicked the switch and the shady yard was suddenly flooded with a glaring light.

In the corner, semi-hidden by the ivy, was a large rock which I had apparently never noticed in the few months that I had lived there.

Whatever Works – July 8th 2013

For me, a huge part of the difficulty in getting my head around the concept of giving up alcohol for good was an idea I had that being teetotal wasn't very cool. Call me shallow for worrying about such a thing, but understanding who we are in and amongst a sea of different personalities and working out what makes each of us as individuals tick, is the key (in my opinion) to for ever sobriety. It is about discovering whatever works, for *you*.

I always defined myself by my hedonism prior to giving up alcohol. Many of my heroes in music and film as I was growing up were drug addicts and alcoholics, struggling with this addiction or that. The music I listened to (and still do) was/is peppered with references to heroin addiction or booze, withdrawals, and lyrics which generally denote vast inner turmoil.

My friends were always heavy drinkers and/or drug users, and a massive part of how I perceived myself was this big hedonistic streak which, for all intents and purposes, pretty much defined me for twenty years of my life, good or bad.

When I decided to give up booze, I was filled with dread that I would become ... (Wait for it, the dreaded word!) *boring*! How would I be able to maintain the persona I had spent so much of my life creating, minus the several-times-a-week alcohol binges?

Well the answer is, I couldn't, which is no bad thing because if you were to ask many of the people who've known me both as a drinker and since I stopped, they would most likely tell you that I was an almighty pain in the arse with the wine in me, and that since knocking it on the head I am not boring, just normal and a lot nicer. There are also, of course, the people who I used to be acquainted with who don't know me as a non-drinker, their patience running out years ago as a result of my perpetual car-crash lifestyle, inability to know what or who I wanted which more often than not led me to hurting those who were trying to be my friend, and simply because they grew tired of being with someone so caught up with wine that she forgot to think about anything or anyone else.

Unfortunately you can't go back, and that damage has been done.

With regards to the 'cool' element of boozy living and whether being a non-drinker can ever bring about that trait, here's what I think about it all now: there is nothing cool about being a selfish drunk who walks all over people and only cares where the next glass is coming from. It is a struggle and a battle and damn hard work giving up booze and staying sober, and reaching that place is a million times cooler than giving into an addiction. And finally, I borrowed a tip from my teenage handbook, and found some 'cool' people who don't drink or do drugs or both, and I use them as my role models. My favourite of these is Anthony Kiedis of the Red Hot Chili Peppers, and if you don't know their music, try listening to 'Under the Bridge' for a bit of motivation and cool inspiration.

It works for me every time I feel a sense of 'I'm just a boring bugger who doesn't drink', coming on, and, even if it's imaginary, I'm going through it all with Anthony Kiedis, which makes it totally cool in my book.

Summer Running – July 12th 2013

I did not feel like running, much, earlier on today – 28 degree heat, a long day working, and a desire to throw myself in front of the TV with a plate of biscuits were just some of the obstacles that stood between me and my fitness, but I forged on and did it anyway.

I remembered this quote from Muhammad Ali, "I hated every minute of training but I said 'Don't quit. Suffer now and live the rest of your life as a champion'," which is somewhat reassuring, I find; if *he* hated training and yet achieved what he did, then there exists living proof that mind over matter works. I might not be aiming for world-class athleticism but I am still striving to be the best me that I can be.

There is a big and gorgeous park at the bottom of the road on which I live and, when the weather is good, hundreds of people decamp onto its vast expanse of grass, set up disposable barbecues, crack open a few beers, and act as if they are on holiday. It has a nice vibe and the drinking never spills out of control – at least not while people are in the park, perhaps later on when they make their way into town somewhat the worse for wear (as I used to do, once upon a time).

I was listening to a varied selection on my iPod from The Beatles to MGMT to Morrissey to the Happy Mondays, (as you can tell, my music tastes are bang up to date) and dragging the dog along beside me, her tongue scraping the floor as she desperately attempted to enjoy this run, something she'd been looking forward to all day but was now finding a little uncomfortable and way too hot.

I ran into the park, just as 'Kids' by MGMT came on my iPod and the sun was burning down on all these people enjoying life and being with each other, and the dog was doing her very best to keep up with me as she panted away like a steam train, and my speed picked up and I was truly in the moment, arms working hard, total rhythm going on … and I filled up with tears that sprang out of nowhere. They stemmed from happiness, and from the amazing world that we live in, and from how grateful I am that I finally, somehow, worked it out that you don't get this feeling, ever, when you drink alcohol.

It was joyous, and I felt totally alive.

Women, Alcohol, and the 1990s – July 20th 2013

The report which was published yesterday in the *Journal of Epidemiology and Community Health*, and which highlighted a worrying trend in women (especially those born in the 1970s) dying at a younger age as a result of alcohol-related illnesses, did not surprise me in the slightest.

As someone who was born in 1975, I came of age around the time of the explosion in both the wine culture in the UK which began with a vengeance in the early 1990s, and the phenomenon that was women drinking in similar quantities to men and subsequently adopting more male characteristics – the 'Ladette Culture' so famously embodied by Zoe Ball and Sara Cox.

It was absolutely *de rigueur* as a young woman circa the mid-1990s to hang out in pubs all weekend, drink pints, play pool, and smoke cigarettes, and that lifestyle utterly defined me from about the age of seventeen onwards, until I became pregnant at twenty-two. In my early twenties and as a new mum I then fell for the widespread marketing campaign of the wine manufacturers, completely buying into the idea that wine was somehow good for us – just look at all those healthy Mediterraneans guzzling their vino, for goodness' sake!

I am not attempting to excuse my personal responsibility here for the fact that I went on to develop a major dependency upon alcohol which was to last until my mid-thirties (I will be forever grateful that I managed to put the brakes on then, and my problem did not escalate further), but I do think that the wider cultural influences that were at play during that era of Oasis and Blur, grunge, a mainstreaming of rave culture and third-wave feminism most popularly exemplified by The Spice Girls and their brand of 'Girl Power,' played a part in contributing to the notion that it was OK for women to drink heavily.

My mindset back in the nineties was characterised by what I recognise now as a false bravado – I presented myself as a hedonist, someone who was always 'up for it' who could drink anyone under the table and beat most blokes on the pool table. It was misguided feminism that propelled me into a lifestyle defined by heavy drinking.

By the time I married and became a mum the habits were deeply engrained, and despite an effort to appear slightly more feminine by swapping the pints of Boddingtons for bottles of chardonnay, I continued to drink, and always until I was inebriated. Because I was already a heavy drinker by the time I had my first baby, the now widely and effectively marketed wine suited my needs down to the ground – here was a sophisticated grown-up drink that I could consume in large quantities but yet remain firmly anchored in what was considered to be perfectly acceptable social behaviour. Nobody was going to accuse me of having a problem with the booze while ever I was drinking expensive bottles of chablis or barolo from Waitrose.

I bought into the wine industry's advertising strategy and felt more than comfortable with being a 'wine drinker'.

Ultimately, I would not have relied on alcohol in the way that I did if my underlying emotional problems had not existed; my terribly low self-esteem and feelings of worthlessness together with the anxiety I experienced in social situations all combined to create the perfect conditions in which a booze dependency might establish itself.

However, if, in the light of the publication of yesterday's report, people are searching for an explanation as to how this terrible situation has arisen where women are increasingly dying in their thirties and forties from alcohol-related illnesses, I would highlight the cultural background of the 1990s as a major contributing factor.

Happy to Be a Non-Drinker – July 24th 2013

When I first decided to stop drinking alcohol, the idea that I would spend the rest of my life feeling miserable as a consequence and as though I was missing out on something was never something I gave much credence to.

Living by a self-imposed regime of teetotalism when my heart was still firmly attached to the bottle, and yet consistently denied its effects, was a prospect too miserable to contemplate. My attitude towards becoming a non-drinker was bloody-minded, and I have remained determined to always continue to seek out the numerous positives to be found in living free from the alcohol trap.

With this mindset, which has now become an inherent part of who I am, I am forever mindful of so many seemingly insignificant events and occurrences that happen each day, which I am fully aware would never happen should I choose to drink again.

Yesterday as I pushed the pram up an almighty hill, hot and tired and feeling the strain in my calves, I suddenly remembered the horrific physical state of being hungover – queasy, sweaty, with stinging eyes and clammy skin, dehydrated, and exhausted in a way that never hits me as a non-drinker despite being up and dressed by 6 a.m. most days. And no matter how difficult that hill was to climb, I just kept on thinking about how awful I used to feel on an almost daily basis – even when simply sitting in front of the TV, never mind pushing a toddler up a steep hill in the sweltering heat.

Last night I poked my head out of our Velux bedroom window shortly before I climbed into bed, and stared for a while at a beautiful yellow moon hanging low in the sky. How many moons, I wondered, had I missed as a drinker when night after night I would either fall asleep on the settee, not even making it upstairs to bed, or was so drunk that I couldn't remember what I'd seen the following morning?

Waking each day and acknowledging the marvel of a fully-functioning memory, feeling no regret or anxiety and with nobody to apologise to for my stupid drunken behaviour of the previous evening, is something I don't think I will ever take for granted. I feel so lucky to be present and to notice all the important things around me, and to be completely in charge of my life and who I am.

For me, maintaining a commitment to sobriety is much less about steely willpower, and more about bathing in the beauty of a life lived untainted by alcohol. I wouldn't give that up for the world.

Sick as a Dog – August 4th 2013

Last night I woke up at 2 a.m. with crippling stomach cramps and proceeded to spend the following two and a half hours ensconced in the en-suite bathroom, grateful for the small mercy that my other half was sleeping elsewhere (when he goes out knowing he will be drinking and coming in after I'll have fallen asleep, he very compliantly settles for alternative sleeping quarters). After collapsing back in bed about 4 a.m., covered in sweat but freezing cold and toying with the idea that I must have picked up malaria somehow, I drifted into unconsciousness for an hour before being woken by the baby at 5 a.m.

Other Half very kindly took over baby duties which enabled me to stagger back to the boudoir, groaning quietly and clutching my stomach. I haven't been able to go back to sleep, hence my writing this now, but I have been lying in bed for a while contemplating the sad truth that I used to make myself feel this way wittingly each and every weekend, and quite often mid-week too.

While a bug of this nature is never pleasant, I am at least comforted by the knowledge that my sickness is purely a horrible piece of bad luck, rather than a dire physical state that I have inflicted on myself in exchange for a few hours of drinking, subsequently acting like an idiot, and waking up only to remember the odd flash of the evening's events anyway, thus rendering the by-product of being hungover as a total waste of my life.

Yes I look horrific, yes I feel as though I have been hit

by a combine harvester, and yes I am suffering from a modicum of self-pity, but at least all I have to contend with today is the illness – the old associated guilt, shame, and battering of my self-esteem are, happily, nowhere to be seen.

I have so much to do today and, as any parent knows all too well, you simply don't get to be poorly when there's a baby to be cared for! So I'll be kind to myself, nibble on a bit of dry toast (is that an old wives' tale or does it work?), and try and keep a little water down, and then I'll get on with my life, albeit in something of a restricted manner.

Once again I am reminded of why life is best embraced minus a drip-feed of alcohol.

In Her Shoes – August 9th 2013

It has been an enormous relief to discover how I truly want to live my life. When I drank regularly and heavily I experienced such a strong sense of being unanchored, as if my true personality had become adrift and was floating fruitlessly, aimlessly, amidst a life that wasn't really mine.

I always imagined that I was a party girl and, when out with friends socialising, I filled the shoes of the token loudmouth, the hedonist, the one throwing pints or large glasses of pinot grigio back while smoking heavily and chatting confidently to strangers. I pursued the rock 'n' roll lifestyle and took pride in my wayward streak.

And yet always in the back of my mind was an idea that I hadn't found 'it' yet, I still hadn't worked life out.

Now that I look back I can see that much of the depression that was once so much part of me, together with my longstanding inability to like myself, came about because I was living like a chameleon with no sense of the person who I actually was. Even worse, I didn't even realise that I was lacking this essential quality, now so glaringly obvious with a sober perspective.

When I look back on it all, it sometimes feels as though I have walked the paths of two people during my lifetime – one who was a cuckoo, albeit a thoroughly unknowing one, and the other the true me who only bobbed up to the surface following my decision to live alcohol-free. Maybe it is similar for those who have shed stones of body weight following years of being morbidly obese; the stretch marks and the memories of being perpetually under pressure to act the part of the 'bubbly' one, the only things remaining of a discarded life once the fatness has disappeared.

I'm not shy but I am fairly quiet, especially in front of those who I don't know very well. I much prefer the company of my family and small group of close friends to being out and about with people who are unfamiliar to me. I hate smoking and I love keeping fit. I enjoy cooking healthy food. I am something of a workaholic, and I'm definitely a perfectionist. I rarely feel stressed. I love listening to loud music especially when running or driving, I can't get enough of reading or writing, and I enjoy being outdoors in the countryside or in a park. I don't mind my appearance but I'm not precious about it at all. My happiest moments are those spent with my children and my partner.

None of the above sounds like the old me, although while I would never want to be that person I once was again, I am not full of bitterness or animosity towards the memory of her. I simply have an understanding that who I was as a drinker only ever existed because of alcohol. If I had never drunk as I used to, the imaginary woman I used to see in the mirror would never have lived.

Most importantly, I'm convinced I wouldn't feel the gratitude for life that I feel every single day, had I never walked in somebody else's shoes. It was a long time coming but I got here in the end.

Booze, Bums, and Tums – August 12th 2013

It's been two and a half years since I cut alcohol out of my life completely. Bearing in mind that one of my very first blogs referred to the switch in my allegiances from pinot grigio to the biscuit tin, and that I piled four stone on in weight during my second pregnancy, it is clear that the issue of my body-shape/size has been ever-present during my sobriety. Like many others, I assumed that a move to teetotalism would result in an instantaneous wasp-like figure, with minimum exercise required and a slackening of the no-cakes/biscuit diet rule that I erstwhile always abided by like a good girl (while pouring gallons of wine down my neck like a very bad girl). Sadly, this was not the case.

So many women write on Soberistas of their disappointment in not suddenly shedding pounds as a consequence to their embracing of AF life, and so I wanted to share this with you – and I hope it offers a ray of hope.

My sober story is not so typical in that just a few months into my AF-ness, I became pregnant. Just prior to the revelation that I had a bun in the oven, and after forking out £100 on a brutal boot-camp course which took place in the park near my home at 6 a.m., three days a week in the dark, I was the thinnest I had been in quite a while. Despite the intense and tiring nature of the boot-camp course, I actually rather enjoyed throwing myself into contortionist positions on the muddy field, especially as I had lost almost half a stone in weight by the end of it.

On the last session I rested my hand on a dopey wasp crawling about on the ground, which then stung me and led to my arm ballooning to alarming proportions. After just half an hour it was the size of a rugby ball. The next day I did a pregnancy test which was positive, the wasp-sting swelling subsided, and I got on with the business of replacing all that lost weight and undoing the toning of my limbs which I had been so delighted with. Within a month I had gained a stone.

I have only recently managed to reduce my weight to pre-pregnancy levels after so much internal battling, over-eating of chocolate and biccies in front of the TV, and double helpings of favourite meals like spaghetti bolognese and Sunday dinners. I felt very strongly for a long time that I was allowed those things as a 'treat' as I no longer drink and my old denial tactics (that proved ultra-effective as a drinker) ensured I hovered around half a stone heavier than I desired until just a month ago.

So what changed? Well I have been super busy, so much so that I actually have not had time to graze mindlessly on Hobnobs. Sometimes I haven't found the time to go for a pee, so biscuits seem to have slid down my list of priorities somewhat. Through being so busy and inadvertently avoiding sweet snacks, I have worked through my sugar cravings without even noticing and, all of a sudden, my head and body no longer scream for chocolate as soon as the washing-up's been done and my cup of tea has stewed and is ready to drink. As a result of the above, I have noticed *results* and lost several pounds in just three weeks. This has spurred me on to eat healthily and to do more exercise, as I don't want to put it all back on again.

It reminds me of all the mental turmoil one becomes embroiled in during the fight to quit drinking. It becomes easier when you cease to be so conscious of it; in the early days it is so prominent in your thoughts but gradually it becomes quieter, less intrusive, and your headspace becomes your own again.

It has taken me over two years to drop that extra weight but I think it would be fair to add at least a year on for pregnancy. At my worst, I was aware of the same self-destructive thought processes with regards to sweet 'treats' as I used to suffer in relation to alcohol, but they have, very suddenly and with no fanfare at all, dissipated to nothing. I now *choose* to eat healthily and not overeat, just as I choose to not drink alcohol.

Be a Part of Something Big – August 14th 2013

In recent years there has been a notable rise of the Soberista, and I'm not just talking about Soberistas.com. Numerous celebrities have opened up about their decision to become non-drinkers and various media worldwide have picked up on the early indications of a wider sea-change in people's attitudes towards alcohol and whether or not they wish to consume it in the same destructive way, something that has become the norm in many parts of the world.

We are used to reading about celebrities who pop into an exclusive rehab for a few weeks after one too many shots of them being completely out of it have appeared in the tabloids, their car-crash lifestyle spilled out for all to see and the subsequent visit to some remote clinic or other becoming common knowledge. But in the last few years there have also been stories in the press about people such as Zoe Ball, Norman Cook, and Daniel Radcliffe who have chosen the teetotal lifestyle but who arrived at that decision with much less of a public display of alcoholic debauchery.

The younger generations (in the UK at least) are drinking less, and the idea of being seen to be openly drunk has lost its appeal for many. Are we beginning to see a shift in attitudes towards alcohol abuse, in a similar way to that which has occurred with regards to smoking?

I believe that for this shift to gather real momentum people need to concentrate on all the benefits of being alcohol-free; this lifestyle choice should never be perceived as 'giving up alcohol', for in using that phrase we imply the denial to ourselves of something pleasant and the focus is fully on what we have lost rather than what we have to gain.

There is only one way to successfully conquer your booze demons, and that is to gear your thinking towards the huge amount of benefits to be reaped by living an AF life, and to not give a further second's thought to the notion that alcohol adds anything to your life. If more people take the bold decision to turn their backs on booze thus becoming ambassadors of AF living, then the commonly held perception of binge drinking being entirely normal and teetotalism being regarded as something only undertaken by oddballs or religious zealots will be increasingly challenged.

If society did not celebrate and normalise alcohol in the way it does currently, I wholeheartedly believe that I would have questioned my wine-guzzling habit many years earlier. In the event, twenty long years passed by before I acted on the suspicion that perhaps all was not well with body or mind due to the alcohol I was regularly imbibing.

Being proud of your AF status is an effective way to contribute to a change which I think has already begun (here's hoping; now raise your glass of elderflower cordial in a collective toast to being a Soberista!).

Conquering a Mountain – August 25th 2013

Three years ago I wouldn't have thought I was capable of running up a mountain that rises more than two thousand feet above sea level. Then again neither would I have considered it possible that I might one day not only stop drinking alcohol but also feel great about making such a decision.

This morning at 6 a.m. I was eating a bowl of muesli by way of sustenance to get me up the mountain outside our holiday cottage. By 7 a.m., we were jogging through a field of cows with the sun casting a beautiful rose-tinted early morning glow all across the valley and rugged peaks laid out before us.

As we jogged upwards through the bracken and occasional sheep, the white houses in the valley bottom growing smaller with every step, I thought about how running up a mountain is similar in many ways to the process of becoming alcohol-free.

There's the hard slog at the foot of the ascent when your legs are growing accustomed to the challenge and the summit is nowhere to be seen – just arduous sidestepping through muddy fields, trying to avoid cow pats and rocks while feeling a bit apprehensive about what lies ahead.

As you get into your stride, the terrain gradually transforms from farmers' fields to rugged mountainside with bracken and boulders all around, and the steep incline becomes more real – you suddenly comprehend the task before you, acknowledging that this climb is going to take every last ounce of strength you can muster. It's tough going; head down, eyes trained to the ground, focus, focus, focus.

Occasionally you stop and turn around to catch a glimpse of how far you've come and even though the view isn't yet at its optimum you know what's coming – the hint of what awaits you at the summit is enough to keep bolstering your efforts and drive your feet further forwards. So on you go, beginning to feel the sensation of achievement.

At the top you get your reward; lying all around is the most fantastic spectacle, you can see for miles. You've never known such clarity, the skies are bright blue, the sea is just visible in the far distance, and the world has regained some perspective – the little things you worried about are no longer an issue and the stuff that really matters is suddenly obvious.

At the top of a mountain, life makes sense.

Back in Character – August 30th 2013

Getting smashed at least three or four nights a week meant that many of the circumstances I found myself in during my drinking days arose out of actions which may as well have been carried out by a completely different person. Looking back on it all, it seems as though I was possessed by someone hell-bent on wrecking all chances of my future happiness.

Certain relationships are top of this list of stupid situations which would never have come about had I been sober. Meeting someone while under the influence when your senses and intuition have been obliterated by alcohol is never likely to mark the sparkling birth of a beautiful romance. Far more likely that the two of you are wholly unsuited to each other, but when morning comes around the process of extricating oneself from such a union is either too embarrassing or shameful to admit to, and so with steely grit you choose to plough onwards and upwards utilising yet more booze, of course, as a way of coping with being involved with the wrong person.

Considering the chaotic life I led as a heavy drinker I can hardly believe that I was the same person as the one I am today. I simply could not see life as it really was, my vision of everything being skewed by a fog of booze and the associated hangovers. The stupid things I said, the arguments I initiated, the embarrassing shenanigans in which I was involved in some effort to play the group clown – absolutely none of them would have occurred today when I am me, in full control of the way I act.

More than anything this total lack of control, which defined my existence during the twenty odd years in which I drank excessively, surprises me. I am by nature a fairly orderly person; I love my house to be clean and tidy, I'm obsessive about work, and set myself high standards in almost everything I do, I can be pretty regimented when it comes to exercise – whether these characteristics unwittingly led me to drinking heavily in the first place in an effort to free myself from the natural rigidity of my character is something which has crossed my mind on more than one occasion.

Whatever the connection, I do know that as a non-drinker I feel happy and contented being in control of my world, insofar as anyone can be. The fact that I constantly used to put myself through the personal trauma of waking up with that awful sinking feeling, as the recollection of the previous night's events came back to haunt me and did so repeatedly thereafter during the following days, weeks, and even months, is enough on its own to account for the serious anxiety and depression I suffered back then. I basically woke up a completely different person from the one I had been the night before – almost every day. That's enough to tip anyone over the edge.

Last night we took the baby to hospital because of a sudden rise in her temperature and ended up staying overnight, me and her snuggled up on a camp bed in a ward filled with crying children and sleepless parents. The fact that I was able to drive her to hospital, comfort her and protect her in such a strange environment, and all the while with the full knowledge that I couldn't have done any more for her, leaves me feeling OK tonight – we are all a bit tired and frazzled but she has fully recovered and is catching up on her sleep in her own bed, and there is no fallout to deal with. It happened, we sorted it, and everything is back to normal.

I dread to think how that situation might have panned out in the old days.

When the Going Gets Tough – September 21st 2013

"I find hope in the darkest of days, and focus in the

197

brightest. I do not judge the universe." – Dalai Lama

I've not had the best of weeks. I'd even say that in the odd, fleeting moment I have come close to feeling depressed, a place I've been lucky enough to avoid for the last couple of years. I have doubted myself, felt powerless and without hope. I've struggled to find sufficient energy to deal with my problems.

For much of the last few days I have been overwhelmed with a desire to keep to myself, to tick along quietly without being bothered by anything else.

It has felt alien and unpleasant, largely because I had nowhere to run, no place to hide. There was no bottle of wine (or two or three) to numb these feelings with. I have simply had to sit it out.

Tonight, some of the perspective has returned and I wanted to share some thoughts with you on how to deal with sadness when sober. Here's what I came up with (and which has helped me):

Don't bottle it up. When you feel down it often makes you want to avoid people, but talking to someone who you trust and who cares will help. A problem shared is a problem halved.

Find some humility. Discovering that you are, in the eyes of others (or maybe just one other), flawed in some way, is not always a bad thing – even if it hurts like hell when you find out. Use it to your advantage and learn from it; it's a good thing to reassess who you think you are. Understanding that you're going wrong in certain areas of your life gives you the opportunity to work on yourself, and ultimately to be a better person. Swallow your pride.

Go for a walk. Being outdoors offers a new perspective on a problem. For me, being in the open countryside (especially where it's wild and rugged) makes me see myself as a tiny part of a vast universe. Nothing shrinks my problems faster than being somewhere that's been battered by the elements for millions of years, and is completely unaltered by humans.

Be strong and dig deep. If you have been a heavy drinker then it's likely you have not developed a comprehensive ability to self-analyse. Drowning problems out with alcohol for years can result in you struggling to pinpoint exact feelings, recognise emotions, and subsequently act accordingly. Learning this skill is at times difficult, and frequently painful. It can really hurt to accept certain truths about yourself but doing this means moving on and following the correct path in life. To know yourself inside and out is to be in charge of where you are headed.

Take a back seat. When you feel down and the bottle is no longer an option for obliterating the darkness, concentrate on muddling through the worst of it by really taking care of yourself. Pamper yourself, indulge in whatever makes you feel happy, eat well – consider yourself to be in need of extra care, and ensure that you provide it as best you can. Take the pressure off wherever possible and allow time for plenty of rest. Tiredness makes everything look a million times worse.

Trust in the following maxim: this too shall pass. It will – things will settle down, the storm will drift slowly overhead and clear skies will return. And when they do, you will have reinforced your emotional strength and there will be no regrets or ill-advised decisions that have landed you in further misery or complications.

There will just be you, as you were before, only a little bit tougher.

What Makes You Happy? – September 26th 2013

"The purpose of our lives is to be happy." – Dalai Lama

Many people, me included, began drinking in the hope of finding a route to happiness. Teenage parties were livened up just as soon as a couple of bottles were introduced into the equation; a Friday night with a friend transformed from merely chatting and watching TV together to uproarious laughter and silliness after a few glasses of chardonnay had been sunk.

We all want to be happy. Life without happiness is a humdrum existence – we are simply being, rather than living. Alcohol for many is the secret to elevating themselves from mundane to extraordinary, the key to flitting out of normality for a few hours and into another world.

We all strive to be happy. We want to enjoy our time on earth.

For me, and I am sure countless others, alcohol provided a reliable, cheap, and easy way to find happiness – for a while.

One of the problems with utilising alcohol as a means to happiness is that the effects are short-lived and, when they wear off, often difficult to remember. Alcohol is also a depressant, and excessive drinking frequently leads to bouts of anxiety and mood swings.

When we choose to live alcohol-free, we lose that fast-track path of transportation to a different place – something which can take a long time to grow accustomed to living without. Gone is the chance to drift away into a parallel universe, and when times are tough there is no immediately obvious escape route. Living AF means learning to live with ourselves, under every cloud, each ray of sunshine, and amidst the most torrential downpours of unrelenting misery.

Despite booze enabling me to feel happy on many

occasions during the twenty years that I spent downing more of the stuff than was good for me, it was a happiness that did not come free from sacrifice. The pay-off for those happy nights dancing and letting my hair down and laughing about nonsense were terrible mood swings, frightening anxiety attacks, and a gradual erosion of my self-confidence.

If the purpose of our lives is to be happy, then for me, this is best achieved through living without alcohol. I can't fulfil my potential when I drink; I am without self-esteem and uncertain of whom I really am or what I want out of life. I stop caring so much about other people and instead am caught up in obtaining my next fix of wine. When I drink, the *only* means of finding happiness (or trying to) is to be found at the bottom of a glass.

Nobody strives to be miserable, and without an alternative common and definitive meaning to life, I will settle on the Dalai Lama's notion of what the purpose of our lives is. I believe that to be truly happy, one needs to exist in a way which the abuse of alcohol quite clearly acts as an obstacle to – to help others, connect with people, care for ourselves, achieve self-fulfilment, find a purpose, and know what it is to have self-esteem.

Transformation – October 3rd 2013

Earlier this morning, I received a follow-up phone call from someone who works at the alcohol advisory service I visited just after I quit drinking in April 2011. Hearing her voice ask me how I was evoked multiple emotions: a real mixture of sadness, delight, and quite a bit of pride.

When I look back on the person I was in the late spring of 2011, I hardly recognise her as me. I recall the only occasion when I visited the alcohol advisory place, shuffling into the driveway with my head hung low, terrified that someone might recognise me. I remember the consultation with the support officer who met me with a friendly smile, sat me down on a chair opposite hers in a dark and dusty room, and asked me to grade my feelings on a scale of one to ten for a variety of statements: I like myself. I have strong relationships with my family. I am happy. I sometimes think about suicide. (The suicide one was high, the self-esteem ones terribly low.)

The walls were decorated with scruffy posters stuck on with Blu-tac and displaying phone numbers and other details of a variety of help centres for drug and alcohol problems. When she asked me what had led me to contacting them I burst into tears and couldn't speak for several minutes.

I never went back after that, despite agreeing to go along to one of the SMART recovery meetings offered at the centre on a regular basis. Whether my decision was based on stubbornness, a bit of denial, or merely because I found it too upsetting being there, I couldn't say – probably a mixture of all three. But I forged on with my decision to not drink alcohol regardless, and here I am now, a completely different person.

I told the person who called me today about the fact that I have set up Soberistas.com, and when she proceeded to quiz me on the scores I would award myself now for various aspects of my life and the state of my emotions, I gave her straight tens. It was a great feeling, like I had graduated from university with flying colours.

However, inside I am all too aware of how very differently things might have panned out for me if it were not for a number of factors. So, to what do I owe my transformation from the alcohol-dependent person I was back in 2011, to the happy and full-of-life person I am today?

I'm very lucky to have a wonderful family and friends who have stuck by me despite everything. Knowing that such a safety net exists has always cushioned me in my darker moments, and perhaps without it I may have crumbled and given into cravings. I am by nature an incredibly determined and obstinate person – I set out to beat alcohol and it would have taken a lot to sway me from this course once I had set the wheels in motion to fight it. The books I read offered me a completely new perspective on alcohol addiction, and they helped me to regain a sense of power in my situation.

Through visiting a cognitive behavioural therapist I learnt that I am not like a leaf blown around in the wind, ending up wherever fate may choose, but a woman with the intelligence, strength, and ability to direct her own path in life.

But most of all, the thing that has helped me to reach where I am today, is Soberistas. Discovering that I'm not the only person (by a long chalk!) who has difficulty in moderating her alcohol consumption, and that some of the awful situations I regularly found myself in when I drank alcohol have happened to lots of other people too, and that the world holds an incredible number of people who are kind and tolerant and full of understanding, has made the last year an amazing journey for me. I really love the Soberistas community and I just wanted to share with you all that today's phone call brought home for me:

When you quit drinking alcohol, you will change. Let go of the fear that you'll struggle to be *you* once you have lost your prop – you won't be the person you were as a drinker any more, it's true, but that's a *good thing*! Without alcohol messing up your emotions and relationships and perspective on life, you'll be free to be the person you *really* are, underneath all of the booze-induced rubbish. Imagine you are clearing a bramble bush to make way for beautiful flowers to push their way up, and allow the true *you* to emerge.

Good things happen to good people, just as soon as you

give them a chance to.

Live Life to the Full – October 13th 2013

It's my birthday tomorrow. I'll be thirty-eight. Creeping up on me over the last few years has been the dawning realisation that eventually (drum roll please), I am going to die.

I have always known this to be the case since I was a little girl, but back then it was the kind of acceptance where mentally you exclude yourself from the situation, i.e. no acceptance at all. We are born, we grow old, we die, but apart from that, I'll be here for ever – gross delusion, one might call it.

Some time around the age of thirty, that all changed. I became deeply aware of my own mortality, a cognition which provided, in part, the motivation I needed to stop drinking. Now, a couple of years of sobriety later, this acknowledgement of my own ultimate demise is never too far from my consciousness. I consider it often and occasionally feel fairly overwhelmed by the force of it. The world will keep on spinning, the sun will continue to rise and set, people will go about their business and build things and have children and go on holiday and buy stuff and take out mortgages and attend school and visit the dentist and the hairdresser, and I won't be here – ever again.

One thing I have realised as an ex-drinker is that regularly quaffing booze acts as something of a barrier to these thoughts. Especially when you drink on a daily basis, the addiction process operates sufficiently well in limiting how far one thinks – the major concern is to make it through to the next drink, thus reducing the scope of one's thoughts, and once that next glass has been filled the mind-numbing process begins all over again. Mornings are adequately taken care of thanks to the low-level but all-too-noticeable hangovers, and onwards the little cycle proceeds. What an alcohol dependency initiates in us is a shrinking of the reach of our minds.

And I often wonder, is this (at least in part) the reason why we, as human beings, have been attracted to mind-altering substances for so many thousands of years? Why so many of us seem utterly compelled to escape our reality, that reality being that we all, one day, will be no more?

Other animals are in the dark with regards to their limited life span. They are not weighed down with the knowledge that their very existence will, one day, be of no relevance at all.

That is, for me, an epic and startlingly difficult concept to grasp.

Without excessive amounts of alcohol numbing and fogging and confusing my headspace, I am a far more profound thinker than I ever was before. And despite the lack of booze resulting in a greater awareness of my own mortality, I believe I am living a richer life, and am filled with a deeper level of gratitude, than would ever have been possible as a boozer.

When I hit the ripe old age of thirty-eight tomorrow, these thoughts will be prevalent in my mind; I am alive and healthy, I have my freedom, I am surrounded by people I love, I understand myself, I know where I want to be and who I am striving to be, I am not constrained by any influences other than those I choose to be constrained by, I learn from my mistakes, I am making progress, I recognise my weaknesses and know how to work at improving on them.

On my birthday I will be intensely thankful for living – and the finite nature of that life makes it all the more valuable.

Where I Once Was ... – October 22nd 2013

My journey began two and a half years ago in the most scandalous place; a curtained-off corner of a hospital ward in Accident and Emergency. My clothes were drenched with congealed vomit. My memory was utterly ineffective in recalling how I had landed myself in that detestable, shameful bed.

The person who had taken me to the hospital was sitting on a plastic chair next to me. He had been driving past my house at 10.30 p.m. the previous night. I was lying on the pavement, throwing up and unconscious, drunk out of my mind. He did what any responsible person would have done, so he informed me – he called an ambulance and then travelled in it with me to the hospital.

I can still feel the sense of shame now if I transport myself to that bed, concealed by the flimsy green curtain. I was a grown woman, a mother, so inebriated that she had been taken to hospital in an ambulance where she proceeded to lie unconscious for hours on end, before finally coming to and facing the truth; alcohol controlled me and I had to escape its grasp before it killed me.

And so my journey of sobriety began. Baby steps; avoid pubs, off licences, friends who drink (OK, all friends), stop smoking – the two things were always inextricably linked – and be kind to yourself. Pamper yourself with beauty products, have a manicure, read books, have restful nights, watch films, spend time being sober with your family.

And then came the internal scrutiny of my behaviour and all those demons. Twenty years' worth of binge drinking to unravel takes time and patience. Weeks become months, moments of panic are slowly lost to the past, downing wine is replaced by other coping strategies; running, yoga, a warm bath, self-help books (lots of those). Begin to socialise again, but now it is different and more to do with the company than the drinking.

The journey is ongoing and will last for the remainder of my life, but I know I'll never drink again. The differences are palpable – no anxiety, no panic attacks, no depression, no mood swings, more energy, creativity abounds, passion for everything – small (jogging in the park early in the morning, just me, the dog, and a rising sun) and large (my wonderful family) – and love for other people, a sense of community.

My journey began in April 2011. Taking the first step on a path to happiness was initiated by taking that final step on a road through hell.

The Other Side – October 26th 2013

My biggest longing back in spring 2011 was to be the kind of person who was unbothered by alcohol, a woman who could happily enjoy life minus the constant buzzing of addiction chattering away inside her head. It was fairly easy to stop drinking in the physical sense for me, but it was an incredibly tough fight to work out a way to feel good about the new life I had chosen.

Never one to do things by halves, I took the bull by the horns and determined to drastically alter my mental hard-wiring. Today, almost one thousand days after waking up in hospital with my mind seriously made up that I would never drink again, I have reached my goal. I have become the woman I set out to be, someone who is happy to live free of alcohol, who never hears the tempting whispers of the wine bottles in the supermarket inviting her back for one final dalliance.

One of the gifts of alcohol-free life is having the ability to perceive the world completely untainted by mind-altering, mood-affecting drugs. The sense of freedom which fills me every morning because I wake up untouched by the horrors that alcohol routinely brought into my world brings about an unparalleled joy, together with the knowledge that I am doing all I can to soak up as much of life as humanly possible.

I have changed from the inside out. I'm still a moody bugger when I've got PMT and I have maintained my irritating (to some) chipper demeanour at whatever ungodly hour I may wake, when I switch instantly from fast-asleep, to Tigger of *Winnie-the-Pooh* fame. I love to cook as much as I always have, I am anally-retentive about cleanliness and tidiness, I love reading classic novels in equal measures to watching absolute trash TV, and I hate – utterly despise – being cold.

But some facets of my personality have altered beyond recognition. In my drinking days I often felt depressed to the point of being suicidal. I was regularly consumed by anger and bitterness over things that I could do nothing to change, and which had happened in the distant past. I was very selfish, I chased instant gratification and fell to pieces when the target of my affections did not transpire to be quite what I had hoped. And I took my life completely for granted.

The world does not become instantly rose-tinted the second one quits drinking alcohol. Instead, the transformation occurs within, and, as in true Buddhist philosophy, there lies the secret to happiness. With a more real perspective, one finds the inner strength to manage difficulties, to cope with life's hardships, and to make the distinction between trivialities and the stuff of greater magnitude. With every challenge that is faced in reality (as opposed to watered down with alcohol), people's emotional core strengthens, and the understanding of themselves, as well as the larger world around them, deepens.

My life now is, without doubt, calmer, simpler, and has little fluctuation from one day to the next. Once upon a time I might have considered it boring to become disengaged with the boozy lifestyle and to reject that wayward inclination I was so convinced was a true element of me. But what cutting out alcohol has allowed me to do is to discover exactly who I am – and, from there, anything is possible.

Life becomes very straightforward if you live it being true to the person you were born to be.

As a heavy drinker who most definitely fell within the 'reckless' category, I would frequently observe people who appeared to be relaxed, full of confidence, and with no obvious need or desire to get drunk. I would wonder how those people could be fulfilled, and ask myself how on earth they managed to just *be*, to plod along day in, day out, never indulging in a boozy evening of blatant escapism. When did they let loose? Was their lack of hedonism as a result of not wanting, or not daring, to let go? How could they be *so* not bothered about drinking?

I am one of those people now. What I could never see back then was that I had created a need for my hedonistic behaviour – it was an artificial reality. The people who I sometimes wondered about – the content non-drinkers – had simply never built up a reason to engage in substance abuse because they had always allowed themselves to live in the real world. As soon as you step into the realm of heavy drinking you lose that grip on reality, and in no time at all your whole existence becomes fake.

In quitting drinking I have planted my feet back in the land of the true, the realists, and the brave. Indeed there are no curtains to hide behind when challenges arise. And emotions are, at times, incredibly painful when experienced in an undiluted form. But always there is a sense of honesty, together with the knowledge that I am doing my best in life.

Put quite simply, if you're after self-fulfilment, I don't think you can do much better than that.

The Sober Revolution Series

Lucy Rocca and Sarah Turner

For more information about **Lucy Rocca**
and other **Accent Press** titles
please visit

www.accentpress.co.uk

Lightning Source UK Ltd.
Milton Keynes UK
UKOW03f0823020314

227422UK00001B/10/P